HANSEN

THE ADVENTURES OF A SURFER, SKYDIVER, TEAM ROPER, ENTREPRENEUR

DON HANSEN
WITH CHRIS AHRENS

Perelandra Publishing Inc.

Copyright 2021 Perelandra Publishing Inc.

Perelandra Publishing Inc
Website: Perelandrapublishing.com
Email: Perelandrapub@gmail.com

All rights reserved. No part of this publication may be reproduced, distributed, or transmitted without the publisher's permission.

Cover photo: Tom Keck

Cover design: Wade Koniakowsky @ Koniakowsky.com

Interior design and layout: Mitchel Shea

ISBN # 978-1-63848-514-8

Printed in the USA by Corporate Color Printing
First Edition

DEDICATION

To my wife and life partner, Shirley, who was there in the best and worst of times. To my children, Christian, Heidi, Josh, and those who departed too soon: Boe, Nicky, and Sage. To my mother, Marie, and father, Fred. To my brothers Harley and Jerry. To my friend and mentor, Bob Driver Sr. To great friends and employees, some who have been here over 40 years. All of you have my endless love and thanks.

HANSEN

The Adventures of a surfer, skydiver, team roper, entrepreneur

CONTENTS

Chapter 1: Redfield, South Dakota   9
Chapter 2: California the Hard Way   29
Chapter 3: Surf Crazy   37
Chapter 4: The Battle of Fort Ord   51
Chapter 5: In the Shadow of Waimea   59

Chapter 6: Surf Biz	83
Chapter 7: The Long Drop	159
Chapter 8: Another Big Sky	185
Chapter 9: Family Business	203
Chapter 10: The Co-author's journey	229

PROLOGUE

The Coronavirus had just hit with every indication that it was about to kick some international ass. All non-essential businesses were closed, and retail sporting goods facilities were no exception. Hansen Surfboards was shutting down for the first time since opening its doors in 1960. Now, weeks before any financial bailout, Don Hansen and his son and store manager, Josh, have agreed to pay employees for as long as they are able.

    I follow Don from his upstairs office through what is usually bustling retail space but is silent and void of customers. Approaching staff members individually, he lays a gentle hand on them with the quiet reassurance that everything will be okay. To him, these are more than just people that keep the store moving; they are family. Hansen's has employed some of them for over 40 years;

others are fresh out of high school. This is their first job, and they fear losing it or something worse happening.

Minutes later, we are upstairs again in Don's office, recording memories of his life while often pausing to laugh at his many adventures and misadventures. With our interview concluded for the day, he asks if I'm afraid of getting the virus. I am in a high-risk age bracket, but honestly reply, "Not really." Hansen, who is 83 at the time, and therefore in the highest risk category, says, "No, me neither." He has faced uncertainty many times before.

In the mid-1950s, there was nobody less likely to become a famous surfer or surfboard builder than Don Hansen. Before he acquired the surf itch, this South Dakota teenaged college student was content to hunt and fish and make a little money as a mink trapper (How many mink trappers have you ever known?) between classes.

There have been a lot of hard-lived, well-lived, joyful, and challenging years between Hansen's teens and today. Still, one thing remains the same: He cannot keep from resetting the adrenaline button for long. At our preliminary interview on April 2nd, 2020, he is limping after injuring his Achilles, post falling into a badger hole while hunting pheasant in South Dakota.

I hate disappointing anyone, but this is not only a surf book. Rest assured, there are enough hair-raising surf stories within these pages for even the most hardcore wave rider among us, but that's only the tip of the tale.

As indicated earlier, like many things Don Hansen ever achieved, becoming a notable big-wave rider in the winter of 1961 defied all odds. He would continue beating those odds while venturing beyond the sea, into the mountains, and as far as the heavens.

While most adventure stories peak before middle age, rocking chair realities never entered Hansen's thinking. Instead, new life has continued being pumped into him like rocket fuel, renewing his energy as he set world skydiving records, attempted downhill ski racing, and won several team-roping competitions.

It's difficult to imagine anyone cramming so much living into so few years. This is the story of a man who carved out his own world, one wave, one parachute drop, and one lassoed steer at a time. In redefining what it means to be fully alive, he has relished some of life's greatest thrills and endured some of its deepest sorrows. In the good times, he has celebrated to the fullest with his family and many close friends. During the hard times, he has held it together by "putting one foot in front of the other," as he is fond of saying.

Those who know Hansen as nothing more than the name on the building of San Diego's most enduring retail action sports store or as a builder of fine surfboards are about to be surprised by what they read. Don Hansen is, of course, a notable surfer with championship trophies and appearances in surf movies and magazines to prove it. He is also a widely respected board maker. Still, to call him a surfboard builder is akin to calling Earnest Hemmingway a typist. The Hansen label is laminated onto some of the finest surfboards ridden on this or any other coast.

Then, right at the peak of his surfing career, he turned to the air, where he set world records as a skydiver. Next, it was off to Montana, where he won rodeo events as a team roper. This book will attempt to discover what drove a kid who grew up 1,600 miles from the ocean to the peak of the surfing world and other equally lofty and unlikely pinnacles. You may be surprised at the adrenaline you can get from reading a story, and like me, glad you didn't have to risk it all to go there.

Chris Ahrens

THREE INTRODUCTIONS

Since this is the story of a man who dedicated his life to excel at more than one pursuit, it seems appropriate there be more than one introduction. Hansen surf team member and surfing legend Linda Benson introduces Don, the surfer and board maker. Skydiving legend Dennis Trepanier gives a glimpse of Don as a world champion skydiver. Montana resident Jerry Pape summarizes Don, his team roping partner with whom he took home top honors.

SURFING

Linda Benson

Linda Benson is among the most beloved of all surfing legends. A big-wave rider, a Makaha surfing champion, and a multiple winner of the U.S. Surfing Championships, her grace, skill, and pioneering work as a surfer, specifically a woman athlete, has opened the door for countless others to follow.

In the mid-1950's I followed my brother and his friends to Moonlight Beach in Encinitas and watched from the cliff as they surfed. This trek would soon change my life and destiny.

At that time, Moonlight Beach was a magical utopia during the summer. It didn't matter if you surfed or swam in the ocean. It was a fun place whether you stayed all day or just stopped by to check it out. The car guys would wax their cars under the cypress trees, and the volleyball court was always in use. The jukebox outside the cafe played "Why do fools fall in love," "Searching," and "Rock around the clock" while young girls danced on the sidewalk. There was something for everyone. It was merely the summer place to go. That's where I first remember meeting Don Hansen. I was around 12 years old and was learning to surf like many other kids. Don was a little older and always friendly with that South Dakota country smile.

 A few years down the line, Don opened the first Hansen surf shop across from Cardiff Reef. All the surfers hung out there, and I made Don's surf team, which consisted of some of the World's best surfers. This was the early '60s, and the next closest surf shops were in San Diego or the Orange County area.

 Getting enough customers to stay in business was a challenge in the early days, so Don had his eye on getting his boards into East Coast surf shops. In 1964 Don, his wife

Sharon, John Peck, and I drove to the East Coast. Around that same time, Hansen's came out with a skateboard line. We hand screwed Roller Derby wheels in the shop's backroom onto wooden decks. This was a huge improvement from the metal wheels we had nailed to 2 X 4's a year or so earlier. L J Richards and Benson Models were sold up and down the coast. I packed as many skateboards as fit into my little red Triumph and took off for my sales trip to the LA beaches.

    As the years and decades pass, Hansen's Surf continues to prosper and grow. His family and long time staff are dedicated to him and their customers. Walking into Hansen's is like slipping on a pair of comfortable shoes. He's not just the owner of a large and incredibly popular local business; he's a friend and has been to generations throughout the county. He has always been generous with sponsoring people, competitions, and many local events. He is still quick to help people.

    Whenever I spot Don up above the sales floor in his office, it's impossible for me not to smile. For so many in the surfing world, his influence and generosity are woven into the fabric of our lives and will be forever. For that, we're grateful. Thank you, Don, we love you!

SKYDIVING

Dennis Trepanier

Dennis Trepanier is a skydiving legend. He first met Don Hansen when he joined "Airfright," a team headed by Hansen that would eventually break several world's skydiving records.

Don Hansen is truly a one of a kind individual. In the entire time I've known him, he has always been happy and enthusiastic about everything he did. I don't think I've ever known someone so passionate and driven toward his goals as Don. He was a spectacular coach who was devoted entirely to the Airfreight Team. He strived to be the absolute best and worked tirelessly, building his team from the ground up. He loved every minute of it. I honestly don't believe you could have found a better person to run that team.

Through thick and thin, Don never wavered. Pressure never bothered him, something that ultimately led to his achieving his dreams of our team winning the Nationals two years in a row. I am truly blessed and thankful to have been a part of the Airfreight team and work with my friend, Don Hansen.

TEAM ROPING

Jerry Pape

Jerry Pape is Hansen's roping partner, close friend, and main antagonist. He summed up their numerous adventures and misadventures with the following few words:

Don and I started roping together many years ago, and from the beginning, we were the oldest guys on tour. We had some great times and many laughs traveling together, but I was ecstatic when he retired because he damn near killed me more than once. One summer, we were competing up in Townsend, Montana. Roping can be dangerous, and to make a long story short, I caught both feet and went to dally [dallying is wrapping the rope around the saddle horn.] He had caught his hand in his dally, and I tossed my rope to him when he hit the steer. But his rope cut his fingers deeply, and his white glove immediately turned red. Off to the clinic where the old doc looked his hand over and told him his middle finger had the skin ripped off. Don impatiently said, "Just fix it good enough so I can play golf." Honestly, he never was worth a shit at golf before or after that, so don't let him give you any excuses. One thing unique about him is that he has no ego, even with all he's done. Then again, he can't have a big ego around me. I know him too well.

CHAPTER ONE

Redfield, South Dakota

The knowledge you get from school is second-hand. The wisdom you get from the sea and waves and water is vigorous, new, and flitting. By all means, get some of this kind of education.

-Tom Blake

The year was 1955. Rebel Without a Cause had introduced American youth to fast cars and switchblades, while the too cool for school vibes emanating from Rock Around the Clock could be heard on six-transistor radios throughout the land. Don Hansen was 18 years old and wanted nothing more than to surf. The problem was the nearest waves at the time were 1600 miles away. A small South Dakota town comes into focus, recalled by Don Hansen.

I had been to California a couple times with my family, and once with a high school friend in an old Buick, my father loaned me. I was a junior in high school, and my dad, who always encouraged my dreams, said, "You guys can take this car and head for California." I think I was 16 at the time, and I drove out there with Jack McDermott, a lifelong friend who eventually became a Wyoming State professor. It was like discovering a new world, and as any teenagers left on their own would do, we stretched the boundaries of fun. We spent a lot of time in the ocean, even though I didn't own a surfboard yet, and so didn't surf much at that time.

After being away for about six weeks, we headed back home. We drove through the northern tier of the country, passing through Yellowstone and Crater Lake before the car

REDFIELD, SOUTH DAKOTA

broke down, and I had to call my dad to send money. But I wasn't thinking about South Dakota much anymore—I knew California was a place I was soon coming back to.

Redfield, South Dakota, is located in the northern plains of Spink County. It rests primarily on farmland at 1,300 feet and lays out flat in all directions. It's only a few hour's drive from Redfield to many historic locations, including the famed Pine Ridge Indian Reservation. The little town is virtually free from modern life's extremes—violent crime and adventure theme parks are basically non-existent. To my knowledge, Redfield has never been featured in a national news story, and it's hard to imagine anyone setting fire to the local police cars.

Still, teenaged Don Hansen's imagination was not stifled by its plainness or lack of apparent opportunity. His fondness for Redfield is such that he continues to call it his hometown and remains in steady contact with many of its residents, including his brother, Jerry. Although distracted by California dreams, Don did what he always did and still does—he made the best of things, all the while keeping one eye down the road for a place compatible with his boundless spirit. As it turned out, no one place could completely contain Hansen's desire for adventure or a good challenge. A joyful, far away expression covers his face as Don tells of his idyllic upbringing.

I was born Donald Milton Hansen in 1936 to Fred Milton Hansen and Violet Marie Hansen in Aberdeen, South Dakota. I grew up 40 miles south of there, in Redfield, South Dakota, where I had my first adventures in the surrounding woods and fields. It was quiet and peaceful during the day, and on cloudless nights you could view the countless stars of the Milky Way. It was Mayberry. Every time I go back there, people recognize me from our high school days nearly 70 years ago.

REDFIELD, SOUTH DAKOTA

We lived on the outskirts of town, around 100 yards from the railroad tracks that led deeper into the countryside. I would walk those tracks during pheasant season, and within a mile, I'd have my limit of pheasants.

Around 2,700 people lived in Redfield when I grew up, and there are even fewer now than there were all those years ago. It was a wonderful life, made better by my family. My older brother, Harley, recently passed away, and my younger brother, Jerry, stayed in Redfield. Jerry still lives there. My brothers and I had many adventures together roaming the plains. We had all kinds of different pets, including the usual dogs, but we also brought home raccoons and a fox.

Don's younger brother, Jerry, recalls their childhood fondly:

There were all kinds of kids in our neighborhood, and we played at different family's houses. We climbed trees and did all sorts of other kid stuff. No matter whose home we were at, their mom would bring us cookies and other treats. We would be playing kick the can when we heard Dad's whistle and knew it was time to return home.

Dad didn't mind running the mill and chicken hatchery he owned, but he wasn't in love with the work either. He had always dreamed of being in the car business. Eventually, Dad sold his companies and bought a Buick and Pontiac dealership in Redfield. He was a typical car dealer in that he was very gregarious. He genuinely loved people, and everyone loved him. Maybe what is not so typical about him is that he was as honest as they come. He was a big man—6'3", 250 pounds most of his life, and bigger than life to everyone in our little town.

Once, when he and my mother came out to visit me in Coronado, he wasn't feeling well. By then, Vince Flynn, whose family I was staying with, was a medical student and knew enough to realize that my dad had kidney cancer. After that, Vince got him over to the

REDFIELD, SOUTH DAKOTA

Mayo Clinic, and it probably extended his life another 20 years. When my father finally died, many people in town came forward to say how much he had done for them. He had made such a big impact on countless lives, not the least of which was mine.

He was good to everyone, but times were different then. Kids obeyed their parents or else. If you did something wrong, lied, or cheated, you didn't have to worry about getting disciplined. You were going to be punished. I remember my dad taking me to the basement with a razor strap, but I don't think he hit me with it. I hated disappointing him, so he didn't have to.

After I began business, I realized my dad was right when he said that customer service was everything. You need to have kind, intelligent people working for you. I always have, and I've never regretted it. In business, I figured I had an advantage over kids raised in California because I had learned to work hard from a young age. Where I grew up, a handshake and your word were better than any contract.

HANSEN

My dad always encouraged me to do what I loved, and I've followed that advice. I've worked in our store for 65 years, and I never have tired of it. Think how productive this country would be if people did what they enjoyed doing, rather than dragging themselves to a job they hate each day.

My father was born in 1904 and lost his own father to the Spanish Flu when he was still a child. His mother died years earlier when he was two. He knew about the hard knocks of life, and he taught me how to cope with them. By the age of 12 or 13, he was flat on his own.

He never went to high school, but he was smart— really one of the smartest men I've ever known. He had more common sense than anybody and could take two and two and make five. With his eighth-grade education, he could outsmart many people with degrees, and he did it with a sense of humor. I'll never forget the time a salesman came by selling aluminum siding. Dad told him, "Oh, I'm really interested, but I want to get this deal signed

REDFIELD, SOUTH DAKOTA

today, so you can get started this week. "The salesman must have become worried because he said something like, "You seem in an awful rush to get this done; is there some problem?" Dad said, "Well, yes, I've just been diagnosed with terminal cancer, and I'm gonna die within the next couple of weeks." Of course, the salesman never returned.

When I was around ten or eleven years old, I worked at the hatchery. I was barely tall enough to reach the trays, and I would "tray" eggs for ten cents a tray, making two or three dollars a day, sitting there for hours. That was my first job, and from there, I went to work for local contractors while still working for my dad at the hatchery.

Our parents gave us nearly unlimited freedom, but they always expected us to return home. Once I left for California, however, I never did come back for good. When I return to Redfield, it looks pretty as it did, and our old house is still standing where it always has. While Redfield remains a nice, quiet place with some of the best people

HANSEN

I've ever known, I don't like looking back. I couldn't stay there because of my love for clean, clear running water. In South Dakota, most of the lakes are muddy, and once I got to the mountains and saw how clean the water was, I realized I had to either be there or near the ocean. Now I enjoy living part of the year in both locations.

We never got into much real trouble as kids, maybe because there wasn't much trouble to get into. We would do the typical things like stealing plums and apples from the trees in a farmer's orchards around town, but that was about the worst of it.

In the '50s, small-town America was fascinated with car culture. Redfield and the Hansen brothers were not immune to its pull.

According to Don's younger brother Jerry Hansen:

Main Street had a three-block stretch, and that where to be seen in your car, driving up and down. We were downtown, dragging Main

REDFIELD, SOUTH DAKOTA

> Street one Saturday night, when one of the headlights in the car began to flicker on and off. Don had no patience for fixing the car, so he bailed, saying, "You can have the car." I found the short in the headlights, taped it up, and fixed the headlights. A few minutes later, Don spotted me and said, "I want the car back; thanks for fixing it," and he was off.

I was eight or nine years old the first time I broke my leg. I was in a hurry, trying to cross the main highway that runs through Redfield, when a car hit me and busted my femur. I would break that same leg twice more, playing sports.

There was a little store called Christianson's Grocery right near where the car hit me. It was my fault, and the driver sat in his car while the owner, Mister Christianson, came out, picked me up, got me off the road, and held me in his arms until the ambulance arrived.

My dad's business was on the main highway near there, but he was at a Toast Master's meeting or something when he got the call. When he heard there was an emergency call for him, he knew right away that it had to be something I did. I don't even remember if they had an ambulance take me to the local hospital—it might have just been in someone's car.

We were always getting hurt, and I still recall being in the basement of our house with my older brother, Harley. For some dumb reason, we were firing pieces of flat shale at each other when one got me right above the eye and cut the shit out of me. Hey, we were just being kids.

I was never afraid of trying new things, and sometimes I would pay for it. I pushed it pretty hard, but I was not one of those guys who are unafraid of anything. I always figured my odds before jumping into the deep end.

As a teenager, I made money doing whatever I could. One job was unloading railroad cars, carrying the cement that came in. I would rent a two-ton truck and go there to unload the bags of cement. I'd hire a kid my age from high school to help. As I recall, those

REDFIELD, SOUTH DAKOTA

bags weighed 92 pounds apiece. There were about 600 bags, and we were able to unload them all in one day. They paid about 120 bucks to empty the entire carload. I'd pay the other kid thirty bucks, it cost me twenty to rent a truck, and I'd make seventy. Shit, that was big money!

We had stacked a bunch of bags in the very back of the truck when I noticed the front end of the truck lifting. When it started leaning to one side, I thought, *What will happen if this thing gets unbalanced?* The truck began leaning further, and I thought, *If the cab of the truck tips and hits the side of the railroad car, I'll owe a lot more than I made today.* I hollered at my helper, and he quickly threw a couple bags onto the front of the truck in just the right place, and it settled right back down without hurting anything.

From my parents, I learned how to work hard and, I still don't care what anyone says; hard work is the biggest key to success regardless of what you plan on doing in life. As well as working hard, I learned to play hard. My father taught me to hunt at an early age, and later on, I learned to trap. Trapping made me a little money during my teens.

I loved playing all sorts of sports, and I lettered in several of them, including boxing. I had three fights one year and *TKOed* all my opponents. The best punch I ever threw in my life was against a high school friend I'm still in touch with. I damn near knocked him out in a sparring bout in the high school gym. He came forward, and I gave him a short little punch that I could feel all the way up my arm. His eyes rolled back in his head, and he started going down, staggered around a few minutes before managing to steady himself on his feet. Our coach, Ken Greeno, who came from a famous couching family, walked right over and made us quit. You were either a man around Coach Greeno, or you were shit. He was a tough old bastard, and he'd get us out there on the field during football training in the middle of the summer heat until we were dyin'. I can still hear him shouting, "Get your ass up and get going!" He influenced my life considerably, and I think many of our school kids felt the same.

REDFIELD, SOUTH DAKOTA

There's another teacher from my high school years I remember for other reasons. Ms. Flora Goddess would come up when you were screwing around and slap a ruler onto your knuckles. She had the same message as Coach Greeno, to get your ass going, but she never used those words. [Laughs] I remember her looking at my fingernails and saying, "*Hmph!* Dirty fingernails and late!"

I was an all-state football player by my junior year in high school, playing wide receiver and defensive end. I hoped to play football at a small college, but that dream ended when I broke the same leg the car had snapped years earlier. This time was worse—it was broken in two places, which ended whatever career I might have had. It was painful and would need surgery, but all I could think to ask a teammate at the time was, "Did I complete the pass?" He replied, "Yeah, you hung onto it." Instead of dwelling on my injury, I changed direction. In the long run, that might be one reason I ended up in the surfboard business.

One of Don's classmates Bill Bacon Bill's remembers Don from their high school years:

We were best friends from the time we were kids through high school. He was a great athlete in all sports, and when we played football, he was the right end, and I was the left end. However, his football career ended when he caught a pass with one hand and was tackled really hard. It was a terrible break of his knee and his ankle.

I think Don's parents always figured he and his brothers would work in their car business one day. But once Don went to California, he got hooked on surfing. Starting from scratch, he built himself a great company. From the time he was a kid, everything he touched turned outright. I don't know how he got into surfing because there are no waves around here for well over a thousand miles.

As I mentioned, I hunted pheasant, and I also hunted deer. Along the way, I somehow got hooked up with an old trapper named Carl

REDFIELD, SOUTH DAKOTA

Santee, who trapped mink every winter. Carl's father was a tough old German man who had been a trapper in Europe when he was a kid. He taught Carl to trap, and Carl taught me.

In those days, there weren't big mink farms like there are now. All the mink in the 1950s were wild. You could get up to 60 bucks for a buck mink, that's a male and 25 or 30 for a female. Carl and a guy named Chuck Badger really taught me to trap—how to make a water set and place it in these weird places or near an old Artesian Well that was still draining water. Once I located a good spot, I would set my traps with fish or whatever I could find for bait. You had to be really careful to stay clear of any other animals when you trapped. It wouldn't harm 'em when they were caught, but sometimes I'd find beaver in my traps, which were illegal to trap. At other times I'd discover raccoons, which could be vicious and could tear you to bits when you went to release them. I accidentally trapped two or three raccoons and even a fox once. I love animals and always made sure to release them without harm. While I did trap as a teenager and have hunted for food occasionally, I now find it difficult to kill anything, even spiders. I trap them in a jar and release them outside.

When I was trapping mink, I'd borrow a car from my dad and take off early in the morning or late in the afternoon to run my trap line. I would run that old car over the fields and, once in a while, get it stuck up to the hubcaps in mud. Then I'd have to call Dad to send someone out. He was easy-going most of the time, but that would really piss him off.

Trapping was a lot of fun, really exciting, and profitable for a young college kid. During semester break, I would leave school to trap for the first 10 or 15 days of the season. I could make four, five, six hundred bucks during that week, which was a lot of money then. The fur traders would stop by my house and buy whatever furs I had.

I graduated from Redfield High School in 1954, but to this day, people who grew up in

REDFIELD, SOUTH DAKOTA

Encinitas insist that I went to school with them at San Dieguito High School. I've heard that so often I finally started agreeing with them. A longtime friend of mine said he remembers me as a troublemaker at San Dieguito. Well, I never went there, and I wasn't really much of a troublemaker. Still, eventually, I started saying, "Yeah, I graduated there in 1954."

I entered college as a math major but soon realized I didn't even know what my instructors were talking about. After that, I switched to a business major. Unlike my two brothers, who ended up with degrees, I didn't stay in college long. I guess I started off okay, though, because, like them, I became president of our freshman class. My brother Harley was freshman class president at South Dakota State. My brother Jerry was the president of the freshman class at Northern State Teacher's College.

Among my fraternity brothers were Pat, Steve, and Vince Flynn. When they showed a home movie of surfing at the Beta House in Vermillion, South Dakota, that was it for me.

HANSEN

It reinforced my decision to go to California. I knew I was not long for school and would soon head west to surf. The Flynn boys said I was welcome to stay in their home, even though I doubt they ever checked with their parents. Their father, Doctor Flynn, was from a family of physicians and a great guy. Keeping calm amid the chaos of raising a family might have been relatively easy for him since he survived a Kamikaze pilot attacking his ship during World War II.

CHAPTER TWO

California the Hard Way

My decision to leave for California was hammered home on a break from school while working to help build a huge grain elevator a couple of blocks from our house. These were the biggest grain elevators in the state at the time, but what I remember most about them was that I was working six days a week, ten hours a day in scorching heat. I'd done my share of hard work before, but when I got my 48-dollar check, I went home, turned on the air conditioning, and said to myself, "I'm not doing this shit anymore." Three days later, I was on the road, hitchhiking to California. All I thought about by then was surfing, and I figured that if I was persistent enough, I could get a job somewhere in California.

Hitchhiking then wasn't like it is now where people are so afraid of one another you would never get a ride. Back then you would often see people hitchhiking to get around the country. I was 19, and while my parents thought I was crazy, they didn't try to talk me out of going. Many of the people I grew up with never left town; neither of my brothers ever did. But they were great, and there was never any competition between us. We simply had different plans for our lives, and it worked out for all of us.

Our family lived about a quarter-mile from the main road where I began my journey. As I recall, my parents drove me there to see me off. I had packed enough food and water for the day along with some clothing and other necessary items in a suitcase. I maybe had a hundred bucks in my pocket. There wasn't a lot of traffic on the road, so I was thankful for every ride I got, even though sometimes I would get dropped off in the middle of nowhere. It was June, but already

CALIFORNIA THE HARD WAY

some of the places in the desert were hotter than hell.

Many times ranchers or farmers stopped for me, but they weren't usually going very far. One guy picked me up in Salt Lake City, Utah, and it seemed like he was going quite a ways. We had driven about 200 miles when his car blew up almost half a mile from a little Utah town called Scipio. The town is still there, and each time my wife and I drive through on our way to Montana, we go past the corner where I sat with my thumb out for half a day.

The town was so small that the car's driver had to wait overnight to get the parts sent in from Salt Lake City. I told him thanks for the ride but that I was gonna keep going. He got kind of pissed at me for that, but I sat on the side of the road, waiting for my next ride for hours. When a carload of kids around my age came driving by, giving me shit, I shut up and tried not to pay any attention to them.

After sitting through a couple thunderstorms, I finally got a ride to Fillmore, Utah. Hitchhiking was slow going, and I had enough money to buy a bus ticket to California. So, I packed up my little suitcase, bought a cheap ticket to Escondido, California, and rode the rest of the way. Once there, I called a buddy of mine who drove out, picked me up, and took me to the Flynn home in Coronado.

The ocean offered a great sense of freedom. Once you got out into deeper water, it was clear. It was freedom in so many ways, and one of the biggest ways for me was freedom from muddy water. Freedom from muddy water; that was one of the main things to me.

I had been in the ocean before and had even surfed a few times. I had mostly bodysurfed then, but after watching that surf film, I knew that board surfing was what I had to do and that surfing would soon become the center of my life.

My close friend, the late George Draper, always claimed he taught me to surf, but I don't think that's how it was. As I recall, my first experience surfing was in 1953 when I borrowed a Velzy Surfboard in Coronado. But Coronado is mostly a steep, hard breaking beach break, and not much good for surfing on the heavy, flat surfboards ridden in the early '50s. Still, it's excellent for bodysurfing. It would get huge near the Hotel Del in the summer, and I was out there swimming into waves with wave faces as big as 15 feet. I recall looking down and saying to myself, *no thanks; forget this.* The first time I got any decent rides board surfing was at San Onofre, which has far more gentle waves than Coronado.

San Onofre was one of the main places everyone gathered to surf, and only San Onofre Surf Club members were the only ones allowed in there. It took years to gain membership. A friend of mine in the club got me right in, so I went to the front of the line.

Pat Curren made my first surfboard, but the first board I ever custom ordered was from Dale Velzy. Both Curren and Velzy are two of surfing's greatest legends, and Velzy could build anything and then sell it to you. When I went to pick up my new board, I couldn't figure out why he insisted on carrying it to my car for me. When I got home and took the board from my car, I knew why— the thing must have weighed a hundred pounds.

I was becoming a surfer, and I let my hair grow down to my shoulders, which identified me as part of the group. This was just before the late 1950's surf boom brought on by the movie *Gidget* where everybody fell in love with surfing and Sandra Dee. There weren't many surfers on the coast before that movie came out, and they all seemed to know each other.

In 1956-'57, I worked for a while at Convair, a company that manufactured aircraft in San Diego. Surf photographer Ron Church also worked there at the time. They would give some of us a little boat to do qualifying dives under the docs in the harbor. We were young, and nobody was watching, so we often headed over to Point Loma to dive for lobster during working hours. I felt ill one day and didn't go with them, but those dumb shits took the boat and got picked up by fish and game for having short lobsters.

I eventually quit Convair to go back to school, this time at San Diego State College. My dad was sending me a couple hundred bucks a month for school at the time, but I quit without telling him. He kept sending me money until about six or eight months later when he discovered I had dropped out. After that, he stopped paying, and I had to return all that money to him.

In 1956 I bought a 1935 Chevy Suburban panel truck. That became my home for a few years. I built a bed, a place to store some clothing in it, and put a little propane stove inside. When I wanted to take a leak, I found the nearest tree. I lived in that truck for a couple years. There weren't many people in Cardiff in those days, and I never had a problem finding a place to park near the best surf breaks, often at Swami's. The local sheriff never did arrest me, but he chased me out every time he saw me parked illegally, and I was forced to move on.

Once, while drinking with the guys down at the old Del Mar Pier, that same sheriff pulled up in his old cop car and grabbed the big bottle of Mogen David Wine we were drinking from. He held it up and said, "Ah-ha, we've got you guys now." He wanted to bust us, but the sheriff with him was more lenient. He knew we weren't causing any real trouble, and he just took the bottle, gave it a toss, and busted it on the rocks. That was a long time ago, and I don't recall who was there with me, but I know for sure we were all underage. We had a lot of freedom then, and age was rarely a limitation.

CHAPTER THREE

Surf Crazy

Jim Fisher was a well-known big-wave rider who lived in Del Mar while I lived in my truck. He didn't care for small waves, and it seemed the waves in California could never get big enough for him. One day when Windansea was big, he and I were out there. I caught a wave and got cleaned out. I was underwater, thinking my board would be right over my head. I stayed down as long as I could, and the minute I surfaced, my board came down and busted my nose. It just knocked the living shit out of me. I must have been pretty out of it because I don't even remember what happened next. Fisher claims he saw me swimming out to sea and that he swam out, grabbed me, turned me around, and said, "Hansen, the beach is the other way." When I finally got to shore, I had a broken nose and was bleeding all over the place. Coronado surfer Johnny Elwell who was standing on the beach when I came in, said, "You're not at Swami's with the little waves now, Hansen." Some of those Windansea guys were friendly, but others were not very welcoming at all. It was always like, "Hansen, you're from South Dakota; what do you know?" They quit hassling me once they realized I wasn't leaving anytime soon.

Palm Springs was the place to be for spring break. Nobody else I knew had a car, so I drove. A couple of guys from La Jolla and Jack Haley [Haley was the 1959 U.S. Surfing Champion who owned a surf shop and later a restaurant in Seal Beach.] I don't remember what we did in Palm Springs, but it couldn't have been anything good since one of the sheriffs ordered us to leave town.

Usually, our out of town trips were to Tijuana, where we attended the bullfights on Sunday. Afterward, we'd hang out at the

SURF CRAZY

"Long Bar," but more often, a place called "The Foreign Club." Surfers from all up and down the coast would gather there. Whenever someone got too drunk and caused any trouble, which was all the time, they'd ended up in the infamous Tijuana Jail. I was thrown into that smelly old dungeon once. It was crowded and dirty, and the floors were covered in water. Thankfully, two Mexican guys who were regulars protected me from some of the more aggressive prisoners.

I was still living with the Flynn family, and, fortunately, their uncle was the head doctor at the U.S./Mexico border at the time. I had been in jail Saturday and Sunday, and when Monday morning rolled around, I thought, *Maybe I can use Doctor Flynn's name and finally get out of here.* I didn't have enough money for bail, and nobody knew where I was because I had driven down alone without letting anyone know.

I told the attaché from the embassy that I was living with the brother of the guy who ran the entire health system at the border.

When I mentioned his name, he asked, "How do you know this person?" He left for about 20 minutes and came back with the doctor I knew, and they let me out of jail immediately. The police chief lectured me before letting me go, saying, "Now, son, you just can't come down here and raise hell like that." The prison staff had taken my wallet, my watch, and all my stuff, but they gave it all back. It was no fun, but it was a badge of honor to have spent time in the Tijuana Jail.

The Stingray that Changed Everything

I was lifeguarding in Del Mar when I spotted a kid in trouble. I could see all these small stingrays in the water, and when I ran out through the shallows to save him, I got nailed on my big toe. I was the only guard on duty that day, and the bleeding wouldn't stop. That evening I was sitting in my truck by the old Del Mar Pier, still trying to stop the bleeding. My friend Bob came by and asked me what was wrong. After I told him what had happened, he said, "Why don't you come by the house, and we'll see if we can get it stopped."

SURF CRAZY

Bob's family didn't live far from the pier, and when I came into the house, his dad, Bob Driver Sr., came out and introduced himself to me. He had gotten out of bed to help me, and I knew right then he was someone special. His full name was Robert Farr Driver, but most everyone called him Bob. I had so much respect for him that I always addressed him as Mister Driver. He was nice to everyone and would often have homeless people in his house, which in a way I was, living in my panel truck. He had been a medic in World War II, and he knew a lot about medicine. After working on me for about an hour and a half, he finally got the bleeding stopped.

I soon became Mister Driver's trusted friend and a friend to the entire Driver family. They were taking off to Europe for nine months and left me in charge of their house. In one day, I had gone from living in a truck to having an entire beach house in Del Mar to myself. Whenever anyone asks if I had any parties there, I look at them and reply, "Are you *shittin'* me?"

Mary Lynn Weitzen is the daughter of Don's friend, mentor, and benefactor, Robert Farr "Bob" Driver. She remembers Don from his years as a Del Mar surfer and lifeguard. According to Mary Lynn:

I was a teenager when I met Don at our house in Del Mar. My oldest brother, Bob, brought Don home. They were friends of the same age and had surfing in common. I remember going with my brother to Swamis to watch him and Don surf. I especially enjoyed that around Christmas when the surf was big. In 1959 my father took the family to Europe for nine months, and Don took care of our house on the beach in Del Mar. I am sure it was the perfect spot to just walk out on the beach to surf, and there were rumors of some great parties.

    I was in high school when Don got drafted and went into the army at Fort Ord. I remember writing him letters—I guess I had a crush on him at my young age. When Don returned to Del Mar with his wife Sharon and their kids, the Hansen family spent a lot of time with Bob's family as both guys were married with kids by then. The kids grew up together, and even my brother's second son's middle name is Don, after Don Hansen.

I think my dad took him first because he was a friend of my brother's. Secondly, because Don was interested in learning what my dad had to teach him about business. Also, my dad was a father figure for Don since his own dad was so far away. My dad was interested in people and never had any judgment toward anyone. He was always ready to help someone in need.

My oldest brother died when he was 34-years-old, and although a son can never be replaced, it was wonderful for my dad to have Don in his life. They continued being close, Don coming over for coffee in the mornings before work for that Father/Son relationship talk. They loved their time together. They traveled together—wives too, and there was so much respect on both sides. They were there for each other in business and through the ups and downs of life. My dad and Don stayed close with their morning meetings until my dad died at age 91. My parents would even have Don's parents out during the winter for a month or so to get away from their cold winters in South Dakota. They also became good family friends. I think my dad saw what a good businessman Don was, and Don listened to his advice, even though they had some disagreements at times. Family came first for both of them, and they both worked hard to create successful businesses.

For the most part, I was responsible and did everything required, keeping the Driver's house in order and clean. But there were those other times... They had this old vinyl-lined swimming pool in their back yard. We had been to Tijuana and brought back a bunch of *Everclear*, which is nearly 100 percent alcohol. We used that to spike the punch we served for our party. I don't remember much of anything after the first few hours, except some of us were launching my surfboard in the pool, trying to surf across it.

SURF CRAZY

When I awoke that morning, I saw bodies sprawled everywhere, and the steaks I had thrown onto the barbecue the night before were just crisp bits of charcoal, sitting right where I had left them. Seeing my surfboard in the pool confirmed that we had been jumping on it, trying to glide to the other side. The nose of a board might have hit the vinyl that lined the pool and punctured it. I always got blamed for it, but I'm not sure it really was me. They were ready to get a new pool anyway.

Ancient Artifacts

My friend Neil Tobin was a great freediver. I was also a freediver, but nowhere near his league. Together we supported ourselves for a couple months one winter, diving for lobster. We'd get up every morning and dive somewhere between Del Mar and Ponto. I remember the water being so clear some days that we'd have 40 or 50 legal lobsters in two hours. Tobin had a big metal pot capable of holding a few dozen lobsters set up in his yard. We would boil them up, and from there, I'd take them on a route I had through Rancho Santa and sell legal-sized lobsters for $15.00 a dozen. We made a little extra money every day.

    I was a lifeguard for San Diego County in '57 and '58. I guarded at Moonlight Beach with Knox Harris, Jim Lathers, John and Bill Hunt, and Fred Ashley. Pat Curren and Wayne Land made boards on the beach behind the lifeguard tower at the time. I didn't often guard Moonlight but was more often assigned to Cardiff Reef or Del Mar. There was a pier in Del Mar before the Under Water Demolition Team destroyed it in '59, the year I was drafted into the army. I once nailed a big sheepshead [fish] with a spear while standing on the pier, 12 to 15 feet above the water. There were never many people on the beach in Del Mar at that time, so we had a lot of free time on our hands. We would surf, spearfish, and dive off the pier. The pier had been damaged during a big storm, so you had to leap across the gaps in the planks that had rotted and fallen in.

    While out diving one day, I noticed this perfectly round rock in 15 or 18 feet of water, right off the pier. I checked that rock

SURF CRAZY

out for two summers in a row, and by the end of the second summer, I was convinced it was manmade. One day I dove down and dug out the sand beneath it with my hand. Then I could see it was a *metate*, a big Indian grinding bowl, centuries old. It had a perfect hole in the center, straight down for four or five inches. The whole thing was sticking up out of the sand.

I had to get it. I borrowed an aqualung, hooked up some inner tubes, dove down, and attached the *metate* to a rope connected to the inner tubes before floating the metate to the surface and getting it to the beach. When I got hard up for money, as I often was in my early years, I sold that metate to a guy for something like twenty bucks. I quickly realized I had made a real mistake selling it, and I often wondered what had become of it. Seven or eight years later, I was driving above Cedros Avenue in Solana Beach and spotted it sitting on someone's front porch, lined up next to many other *metates*. I stopped, and sure as hell, it was the one I had pulled out of the water years earlier. I knocked on the door, and Craig, the guy I had initially sold the *metate* to, answered. I said, "I'm Don Hansen, remember me?" He said, "Yeah, sure, I do." When I asked him if he wanted to sell that *metate* back to me, he asked how much I would give him for it. I think I paid him 50 bucks to get it back. Shit, I wouldn't sell it for five thousand dollars now; it's priceless. The Scripps Institute of Oceanography did an article on it once, saying it was the biggest, most perfect *metate* ever found around here. I have it sitting on the fireplace in my house, filled with pennies. [Laughs]

After getting that first one, Tobin and I would often dive for *metates* together. Neil didn't surf much, but he was a fantastic diver. I think he was with Jose Angel when Jose died diving for black coral in 200-some feet of water in Hawaii.

My goal in working was never to get rich, but simply to survive and have enough money in my pocket to not become a drag on other people. I always said, "Work to live;

don't live to work," and that's the way it's been with me all my life. Some jobs weren't so enjoyable, like working as a pool builder for about a year. There's nothing hotter than being at the bottom of a swimming pool in the summer when the sun is focused directly on you.

Living was easy and inexpensive in those times, especially when you didn't have to pay rent. With the beach towns in the North County of San Diego having such small populations, it was always easy to find a place to park my truck and spend the night. Cardiff, Del Mar, Solana Beach, Leucadia would roll up the sidewalk after five or six in the evening. Nothing was open except for one of the little bars each town had. Highway 101 would never be crowded until summertime, and then it was jammed, bumper-to-bumper for miles because the freeway had not yet been built.

CHAPTER FOUR

The Battle of Fort Ord

Not long after moving from my truck into a little house with three or four other surfers, I got my draft notice. I wasn't worried about it because I had previously taken a pre-induction physical and was told I would probably be classified 4-F because of my leg. I was ordered to report for a second physical and figured I'd be going right back home afterward. Instead, the draft board said I was fine, and that same night put me on a train headed out of San Diego to Fort Ord, which was just north of Monterey, with about 500 other guys.

    The keys to my truck were still in my pocket, so I called my girlfriend and asked her to hotwire it and drive it home. I told her to go to my house and get my stuff before my roommates realized I had been drafted and began dividing everything I owned between themselves, which they had already done by the time she arrived. [Laughs]

I was in the military until 1960, but I was never anywhere near combat. I was a clerk typist, fighting the battle of Fort Ord for two years. People who have been in battle tell me you never know what you'll do until the bullets started flying. While I never wanted to go to war, I always wondered how I would react to it.

Whenever I got a pass from the army, I would drive to Santa Cruz to surf the great waves at Pleasure Point or Steamer Lane. That's where I first met Jack O'Neill. Jack was a great guy, but not much of a surfer. Still, whenever the waves got big, he was out there. Jack was a surfboard maker at the time, but his shapes weren't exactly great. When I met him, he was more interested in the wetsuits he would later become famous for than building surfboards. I had never made a board before, but I had owned boards

THE BATTLE OF FORT ORD

made by top shapers like Pat Curren and Dale Velzy. I knew what a good board should look like, and Jack's boards were lacking. When I told him I wanted to shape for him, he gave me ten blanks and said, "Here, shape all you want." I was a good enough craftsman that I learned to shape on my own pretty quickly.

I made some surfboards and many good friends through surfing in Santa Cruz, including Johnny Rice. Johnny was a great surfer who became a quality board maker, and he eventually nominated me into the Surfboard Builder's Hall of Fame. I've been inducted into two or three halls of fame, but most of them went bankrupt. [Laughs] It seemed that whenever I hung around with Johnny, he got me into trouble. Maybe it was the other way around at times, but I doubt it. He was such a colorful character and had done so many different things in his life. I heard he became really good at karate after getting the shit beat out of him a couple of times in Hawaii.

Jack hadn't developed a good surfing wetsuit yet, and the water was cold. Sometimes we would paddle out in a sweatshirt or something, which didn't work very well once it got wet. Still, the surf made it worth it, and Steamer Lane got big at times, which proved good practice for the North Shore, a place where all surfers eventually end up to prove themselves.

Bob Bermel was a surfer stationed with me at Fort Ord. He had been among the first crew to surf Waimea Bay in Hawaii. This night though, he distinguished himself along with me by getting thrown into jail. I was driving back to Fort Ord after an evening in Santa Cruz. It was really foggy as I whipped my way through the artichoke fields. I was focused on driving down the white line, trying to stay out of the fields when I ran a cop car driving in the opposite direction, right off the road. We ended up off the side of the road ourselves, in a ditch. I can still remember Bermel saying, "Don't worry, Hansen, they can't arrest us." As the cops pulled us out of the car, I said, "Bob, shut up" before they took us to the Salinas Jail.

THE BATTLE OF FORT ORD

They gave us these thin mattresses that most everyone placed on the cold cement floor. Instead, I threw my mattress over me, trying to stay warm. When someone's arm came over my hip, I said, "Hey, buddy, get away from me." I thought it was Bermel screwing around until I heard him from the other side of the cell say, "Hey Hansen, it isn't me." Everyone in the cell howled with laughter.

The opposite feeling of going to jail is getting a new surfboard. I was stoked to try out the brand new board I had made at O'Neill's. I took it down to Pleasure Point, paddled out, and lost it. I was only about ten feet away, just about to grab it and paddle back out when another wave hit. There was a sharp rock on the beach; my board hit it, it flipped up and broke entirely in half. Not such a great day after all.

Soon after my discharge from the army in 1960, I married a woman I had been going out with, Sharon Anater Kovalenko. We had a small service in a little church in town where longtime Santa Cruz surfer Jerry Colfer served as best man. Sharon was a surfer with two children: Nicky and Boe. We ended up having three children of our own: Christian, Heidi, and Sage, AKA Donald Milton II.

I began taking Sharon out about four years after she had been divorced. Her ex-husband, George Kovalenko, was a Santa Cruz cop, and he was apparently still in love with her. For obvious reasons, he didn't like me and wanted to arrest me, or at least get me out of town.

I had rented a house in Santa Cruz, and we were having a big party there. That's where I first met Mike Doyle, a man I would later enjoy working with and who would have a significant influence on me. Doyle had gone into one of the bedrooms and was either asleep or had passed out. When the cops raided the house, I ran into the bedroom, dove over Doyle, and said hi before running toward the window and diving right through the screen. I landed in the backyard, where I took off running. I

THE BATTLE OF FORT ORD

was the one renting the house, so I would be the one in trouble if I were caught. It was two or three more hours before I returned home. By then, everyone was gone. Narrow escapes would come in handy in the waves I was about to encounter.

CHAPTER FIVE

In the Shadow of Waimea

I arrived in Hawaii in the fall of 1960 after a 12-hour flight on "Pleasant Hawaiian Holiday's" flying out of San Francisco. Flying there and flying back, I kept wondering where all the gas was coming from to stay in the air that long.

Seeing Oahu from the air for the first time was one of the most exciting points of my life at that time. It looked so peaceful and inviting from the air. Still, I knew it wasn't as tranquil as it appeared and that I was about to be challenged by the biggest waves ever ridden at the time. Everyone was talking about these newly ridden spots Waimea Bay and Pipeline.

Upon landing, we noticed the humidity was suffocating, which was something we soon got used to. I didn't know famed Hawaiian surfer Sammy Lee at the time, but he remembers seeing me get off the plane. He was working at the airport then, and he told me years later that he had seen me with a pregnant wife, two kids, and half a dozen surfboards. I had made the boards while working for O'Neill, and my plan was to sell most of them and live on whatever came in for the first few months. Lee said he wondered where the hell I was coming from and where I could possibly be going, and I kind of felt that way myself.

After getting a ride to the Mile of Cars in Honolulu, we bought a 1946 Studebaker for about 300 bucks. Many visiting surfers lived in their cars back then. I wouldn't have minded that, but it was out of the question with two children and a pregnant wife. Like most everyone else visiting the North Shore from the Mainland at the time, we lived some-

IN THE SHADOW OF WAIMEA

what primitively, in whatever shelter we could find. We didn't have much that year, but this would become one of the most fun and adventurous periods of my life.

Oahu was beautiful, but I wasn't there for the scenery; I was there for one reason—to ride the biggest waves I could find. I was determined to charge whatever came in, but I still wondered if I was up to the task.

I don't recall where we stayed that first night or if we had already reserved a place in Kawela Bay, which would be our home for the winter. Anyway, we ended up renting a place in Kawela Bay, just north of Sunset Beach. The Kahuku Sugar Plantation owned these old plantation houses. I recall that the foreman who rented to me was named Morgan. I had called him up and asked if he would rent us one of his cabins. Without knowing anything else about me, he quickly agreed. The rent was forty or fifty dollars a month.

If you didn't know where Kawela Bay was, you would not even know it was there. The area was overgrown, and you had to take a little dirt path to get in. Once you did, it was a paradise. A few years ago, I was looking for the road again, and I asked a guy at his vegetable stand on Kam Highway where the entrance was. He showed me, and I drove down the dirt track to the place our family had once lived. Our house and all the other cottages were gone. Other than that, it was the same Eden it had always been.

We first arrived there in fall, which is early for the big-wave season. There weren't many guys surfing there yet, but it turned out that the surf would be excellent early that year. The only surf photographer around was surf filmmaker Grant Rohloff.

One of the first places I surfed was Chun's Reef, a Southern California type of wave. As I mentioned, I was always attracted to clear water, and it was so clear I could see down to the reef at Chun's all the way to the outside. Clear, warm water, uncrowded, perfect surf. I was in heaven. I had only been surfing four or five years by then, and there were many better surfers than me in the Islands at the

IN THE SHADOW OF WAIMEA

time. I was in awe of my surroundings and would soon be in awe of how massive the waves could get at times.

After a short while, our kids began looking like something out of Tom Sawyer, all tanned with sun-bleached hair, never wearing shoes, shirts, or anything but shorts. I wasn't interested in fruit at the time, but there were all sorts of wild guava, breadfruit, and mangoes free for the taking. We lived on a lot of rice and lobster. There were some shallow spots in the middle of the bay where you could always count on getting enough lobsters for a meal. It was also legal to take turtles in those days, but I never got any of them. Two of the best divers I had ever known, Neil Tobin and famed big-wave surfer and deep-water diver, Jose Angel, came by one day and took me to another reef. It was really shallow for about a quarter-mile before it dropped off into deep water. After we got chased out of the water by a big shark, we ended up swimming inside and hanging out in the shallow part of the reef.

My car only broke down once when the rear end went out. Then, my friend Neil Tobin, already on the North Shore, and I scoured the ditches along Kam Highway for abandoned cars. Neil was great at fixing cars, and when we found a junked Studebaker in a ditch on the side of the road that was similar to mine, we went to work. The vehicle we located was covered with dirt and weeds, and I'm not even sure it was the same year as mine. Still, we jacked it up right there and removed the needed parts while the locals drove by, screaming out, hey, *haolie!* Once we removed the rear end, we replaced it with the one from my car. It went just fine from then on, and I ended up driving that car every day for the remainder of that year without any more problems.

Paradise Found

Tom Keck is a photographer and a good friend of mine from Coronado. In 1960 he and John Elwell were going to school in Hawaii at Brigham Young University. Tom had rented one of these old plantation houses in Kawela

IN THE SHADOW OF WAIMEA

Bay near me, and he let me make surfboards in the garage attached to his place. He said he didn't want to leave his car in the garage because it was so dilapidated the roof might fall in and damage his car. Thanks, Tom. [Laughs] According to Keck, "The place was so full of holes that there was foam dust flying around everywhere when Don was shaping."

The houses had no windows—just screens and shutters so you could board everything up when it rained, as it so often does in the Islands. You could barely call it a house, really, but it had everything we needed, including an inside toilet and a sink. Other than that, it consisted of one big bedroom and was just open.

I was 26 years old at the time, and while not everyone would have liked living where we did, my wife Sharon and I loved it. Nicky was probably four or five, and Bo was around seven at the time. They were too young to surf over there, but they spent hours each day exploring the beach and shallow water near the reef.

HANSEN

The founder of Surfer Magazine, John Severson, arrived sometime before Thanksgiving to take still photos for his magazine and shoot film for his surf movies. He lived just down the road from us. We went to his house on Thanksgiving Day, and I brought a turkey. He also had a turkey, but he served mine and kept his. Food was scarce in those days, especially with a wife and two hungry kids, and I was hoping to go home with some leftovers. John and I were friends, but that kind of irritated me for a while, especially since he had a lot more money than I did at the time. Like most everyone else who had migrated to the North Shore to surf, we were living on a shoestring. It didn't cost much to live, and I made a little something on my surfboards. Still, we needed a little more to survive. That was the only time in my life I collected unemployment.

Severson made up for everything and more when he put me on the cover of Surfer Magazine. I wasn't much of a small-wave surfer, but being on the cover riding Haleiwa was a pleasant shock to me. There was very

IN THE SHADOW OF WAIMEA

little surf media around in those days, and Surfer was the leading magazine. If you got your photo on the cover of Surfer Magazine in those days, you were made.

I was determined to surf whatever waves came through while many of the guys sat on the beach when it really got going. I understand that, and I can't blame them; it can be terrifying. I was scared at times, but I always tried to make it out, even though I had my heart in my throat a few times when I got stuck inside on big days at Sunset or Waimea. Keep in mind that they measure the wave from the back in Hawaii, so when what they call a 15 to 18-foot wave is dropping on your head, you're nothing. You quickly realize how small you are compared to the ocean that is trying to hammer you.

You'd be out trying to get over to the channel when you spotted something coming in from way outside. Suddenly there'd be this vast wave face about to break on you. Your adrenaline is pumping, and you have no choice then but to push your board away and dive as deep as you can. If you were lucky, your board made it over, and there were no bigger waves coming in as you paddled out into the lineup. I had some shots of myself riding big waves in some of Rolhoff's movies—*North Swell* was the main one, and if you can find a copy, let me know—I'd love to see it again. Grant knew I was making surfboards, and he always did his best to help me out by getting me into his movies. When he aired the film, he'd give my business a plug by saying something like, "Here's Don Hansen riding one of his own surfboards." That really helped my business eventually.

Tobin didn't board surf much, but he was a hell of a bodysurfer. He showed me some of the breaks, but I mostly learned them by watching for a while and figuring out where everything was in the lineup. From there, it was just paddling out, getting into position, and go. Going was not always that easy, especially at Waimea, which is a lot more challenging to ride than Sunset.

IN THE SHADOW OF WAIMEA

For me, it was mostly a survival stance, and once you came out over the end of the wave, you breathed a sigh of relief that you had made another one. The worst part of it was the anticipation and wondering what might happen if you got caught inside. You knew the waves were going to be massive as you drove down Kam Highway to Waimea. Every other North Shore big wave spot like Sunset broke way out to sea and closed out, sometimes flooding the road with the surge. Once I got down to the beach, however, I knew I was going out there. I never did work out, but I surfed all the time, watched my diet a little, and I stayed in reasonable shape.

I made a 10' 6" elephant gun for a local surfer named Max Lim. I was in my mid-20s at the time, and he was around 60 and still riding big waves alongside us. He was a fantastic surfer and a really nice guy. Randy Rarick recently told someone he located that board and sold it at auction. He said the words on the stringer read: "Elephant gun for Max

Lim." I wish I had known that board was for sale; I would have paid good money to get it back.

There were some big days at Waimea that year, and one of the biggest compliments I ever had in surfing was after I came after riding a big day. The waves were massive, and there were a bunch of guys sitting on the beach watching. As I walked by, one of the guys, Ricky Young, who was among the better surfers coming out of South Bay, said, "Well, Hansen, you rode some big waves today; you no longer have to prove yourself." I don't know about that, but I know that I have this habit of doing something as hard and as well as I can for a few years before moving on to the next challenge. I didn't quit surfing after that winter in Hawaii, but I was never again as into it as I was that year. There were other challenges ahead and other things I wanted to try.

Greg Noll may not have been the most stylish surfer in the world, but he sure looked good to me, and he took off on anything. No

IN THE SHADOW OF WAIMEA

wonder they call him "The Bull." Some guys like Noll don't seem to have any fear; they just aren't afraid. Like anyone who's lived life over the edge [the name of his biography], Greg has had some close calls. One was at massive Makaha in 1969, where most agree he rode the biggest wave ever up to that time.

Some guys die pushing the envelope that hard, and while surfing big waves can be an adrenaline rush and scary for sure, it's usually not life threatening. Even so, I have no trouble admitting that everything from big wave surfing, skydiving, and team roping has scared the shit out of me at times. In surfing, I got to the point where I reached the peak of my own performance and thought, *I don't have to do this anymore.* Maybe it was as Young said, I no longer had to prove myself.

Greg Noll, Pat Curren, Dick Brewer, and Mike Doyle were some of California's standouts when it got big. Kimo Hollinger, Henry Preese, and Jose Angel were among the prominent locals. Angel was a fantastic surfer and diver, and I never heard him brag about anything he ever accomplished.

HANSEN

If you lost your board, you had no choice but to swim for it. You hoped you weren't right in the "kill zone" where the waves could drive you to the bottom. That was the only thing I was afraid of. I always tried to get in further or out on the other side of it.

The surf leash wouldn't be invented for another decade, and when you lost your board, you were in for a long swim, especially at Sunset. When I lost my board there, I'd get into the reef where it was only a foot or two deep. I must have had a lot of adrenaline running through me because once I got there, I'd run over that reef, cutting the shit out of my feet without really feeling it. That channel would be running like a river, and I'd make sure I was as far to the north as I could get before I dove in and swam like a son of a bitch for the other side. I'd pray I'd get in before the channel turned into a rip and headed out to sea. When someone got caught in that rip, they could be taken out 300 to 400 yards in like five minutes. Then you'd hear them yelling, *Help! Help!* If you didn't get your board

IN THE SHADOW OF WAIMEA

right away, you'd have to go around again. Sometimes someone's board would get swept out to sea, and the owner would ask you to go get it. Not a chance!

I never did any training for big surf, but having surfed in Santa Cruz for two years, I was used to being in some pretty big waves. Even though Santa Cruz waves didn't have Sunset's power, there were other challenges to face. At Steamer Lane, you had to deal with the cold water, thick kelp, sea lions barking at you, and the ominous sound of foghorns. The water in Hawaii was warm and clear, so the surf's size never bothered me that much initially. It wasn't until later when you realized how powerful some of those waves were that it kind of scared you. You're a little bit of nothing out there. You can't hang onto your board; a big enough wave will rip it out of your hands. If you're smart, you push it away and swim. I was in the best shape of my life, and I was a decent swimmer, so I knew I could always get in.

HANSEN

The ocean was not the only place you might face danger in Hawaii—you could find it just as quickly on land. I always figured you needed someone to protect you when you were on the North Shore, and Henry Preese was my primary protector over there. He was such a great guy. I'd be out drinking with the guys, and by the end of the night, after the local boys had a few, you were a *haolie*. Whenever one of the Hawaiians would say something about me being *haolie*, I wouldn't respond, but Henry would jump in and say, "Leave 'im alone; he's my brother." I always stayed in my place around the Hawaiians; I was very aware that it was their island, and I gave them the respect they deserved. Even so, sometimes, after a few drinks, you could instantly become the *haolie*. Henry saved me more than once. I also made sure to be friends with Rabbit Kekai and Buffalo Keaulana. They were like royalty, like Hawaiian chiefs, and everybody respected them.

If you wanted to surf Makaha, you needed to know Buffalo. Rabbit is gone, but he and Buffalo were among Hawaii's greatest surfers, and there is so much respect for them in the surfing world. Many years after my first trip to the Islands, I sent my son Josh there. He was young, and some guys began hassling him in the lineup. I called Rabbit and told him about it, and he said, "Don't worry; I take care of it." That was the end of that.

The Hawaiians didn't come over to the North Shore much in those days. I don't think they were as serious or as competitive as the Mainland surfers were. While they were mostly naturally gifted surfers, most of them surfed merely for the joy of it. Some of them claimed they were the first to ride the Pipeline. Maybe so, but it's hard to imagine riding that place with ancient surfboards.

If you didn't live right on the beach, the only way to know when the surf was huge was when you felt the ground vibrating. Then I'd think, *Shit, now I've got to go down to Waimea and paddle out.* I always went out, and I got some big waves there a couple of times. Still, you have some anxiety attacks.

HANSEN

A typical day at Sunset, at least for me, was riding four or five waves. It's a long way out and a lot of paddling. After four or five waves, I'd be done. The scariest part there is when the peak shifts and you're about to have a big wave break on you. Then you'd find yourself scrambling to get up and over the top. If you don't make it, it's a long trip over the falls. I never did get sucked over the falls, but there were times when I was paddling for a wave and got sucked back up into the crest with the offshore wind blowing into my face. I wasn't always sure if I was gonna make the drop or not, but to my recollection, I always did.

One morning I awoke to feel the ground shaking, and I knew the surf was really big. There had been a party the night before, I had a terrible hangover, and I thought, *If I have to surf today, I'm gonna die.* [Laughs] But true to the promise I had made myself, I loaded up my board and drove to the Pipeline. I had never seen Pipe that big, and I can still envision Greg Noll standing there when John

IN THE SHADOW OF WAIMEA

Severson took what would become one of the most famous surfing photos of all time. Greg was contemplating how to get out, standing alone with his board leaning against his shoulder as the waves roared in front of him. The photo was taken just before he paddled out and rode what was probably the biggest surf ever ridden at Pipeline to that point.

I may have been too hungover cuz I had always been able to get out before. However, this time, each time I tried paddling out, I ended up way down the beach. After my third time getting washed down the beach, I watched a couple of massive waves come through. I thought, *Do I really want to go out there?* That was the only time I backed out. In surf that size, you gotta know when to say no unless you want to die.

I eventually *did* surf Pipeline on some smaller days. It can be dangerous, but almost everyone survives. Still, once in a while, someone will die trying. The waves they're riding now are far more dangerous than they were then, like the one woman who recently rode a massive wave in Nazare, Portugal. They say it was the biggest wave ridden that year and that it measured 75 or 80 feet. That's hard to imagine because if that thing really steepened up and came over on you, it could kill you.

When you're out there on a big day, you realize the ocean can eat you alive. The only photo I have on a big day is at Sunset on one of the smaller days that year. Judy Rohloff, Grant's wife, took the shot. It measures out a lot bigger from the face, but if you consider it from the back the way they do in Hawaii, they would probably only call it around 12 feet.

To my knowledge 1960 was the first year some of the Aussies showed up in Hawaii. Mick McMahon, Midget Farley, maybe Nat Young, and some other Australians whose names I have forgotten lived just down the street from us. They were all great surfers, and it was fun talking to them about their homeland. They would pave the way for those who came later and would eventually make their names in

IN THE SHADOW OF WAIMEA

Hawaii. Back then, however, they were just getting started.

When you're in the lineup on a big day, the first person to see the set coming starts paddling out, and you think, *Oh shit, I gotta get out of here fast, or else...* You're racing to make it, and when you finally paddle into the right spot and take off just right, it's very satisfying. When you see that wave coming, you want to make sure you're in the right place to drop into it. You can't be too far in or too far out. Once you start paddling, you quickly discover if you're in the correct position or not.

There were board builders in Hawaii since ancient times, but by the time I got there, I looked to see what top shapers like Pat Curren, Joe Quigg, and George Downing were doing. It was just that much more exhilarating, riding a board you made. I was probably making aboard a week for a while. When you create boards for big waves, you need to have confidence in them. Either that or you'll be swimming all the time. I had confidence in my boards—they were long and narrow and heavy enough, and I knew they would work in any conditions. I was building about one board a week, even though it wasn't that profitable, and I brought in less than $100 a week. Even back then, that wasn't sufficient for a family of four, which was soon to be five. That's okay; no amount of money could buy what we had.

Greg "Da Bull" Noll is ranked among the greatest big-wave pioneers of all time and Hansen's close friend.

According to Greg Noll:

> I first became aware of Don Hansen while surfing Haleiwa with Bruce Brown and many of the North Shore crew that year. He was a good surfer, not like Phil Edwards. Still, he could surf, especially for having come from South Dakota or Kookamonga or some shit. He became part of our group right away. Some guys never make it, some guys kind of teeter,

and some guys fit in. Hansen was one that fit right in. When I got to know him, I realized he was a really neat guy, and I would now put him in the top ten of my really good friends.

Don paid a lot of attention to detail when he made surfboards. He prided himself on knowing everything that was going on. Once, however, after we returned from the Islands, Australian [Bob] McTavish had introduced the world to shortboards. I got an order from Charlie [Big-wave charger and Noll shop manager in Hawaii, Charlie Galento] for 150 shortboards. They were little tiny boards, all-around seven feet in a time when boards averaged around ten feet in length.

Hansen came by to visit, and he wanted to have lunch. He kept heading for the door of the factory, and I'd block him off. Finally, the telephone rang, and he got by me, and I heard this "Holy shit; what's going on!" There were like 75 racks with all these shortboards in them. That was the first time I ever saw him caught with his shorts down. It was neat to catch him unaware.

    Hansen and I were in Puerto Rico for the World Contest in 1968. We went out and got drunk together, and he stuck his tongue out at me. I reached over, grabbed his tongue, and held on really tight. He was squealing like a pig. All he had to do was chomp down and bite my hand, and I would have let go, but he didn't, and I hung on. He was a bit of a goodie two shoes, and my friends and I were kind of scum of the earth, but somehow we became great friends. All I can say is good shit about Don; just tell him not to stick his tongue out at me anymore. In the end, all I can say is that the world's a better place because of Don Hansen.

CHAPTER SIX

Surf Biz

"Don't let anyone tell you that luck doesn't have anything to do with success, because it does."

La Jolla surfer Bill Thrailkill worked as a shaper for Hansen in the mid-1960s. According to Thraillkill:

> I was shaping for Hobie in 1965 when Don asked me to shape for him. My friend Ronnie McLeod became the glosser, and I was one of Don's shapers. Hobie paid eight dollars a shape, and Don paid ten. I was doing five boards a day, so that was decent money in those days. Don was a very gracious guy and a stickler for quality, but I could see that

HANSEN

Hansen was phasing out of surfboards by 1969.

Once the big wave season ended, we figured it was time to head back to the Mainland and make a go of the surfboard business, even though we had no idea how that would pan out. Hap Jacobs was a really nice guy and owned one of the biggest surf shops on the West Coast, Jacobs Surfboards. He had once been a partner with Dale Velzy, and he said he would pay for my family and me to get back to the Mainland if I would shape for him. I agreed and once again found myself on a Pleasant Hawaiian Holiday's prop plane for 12 hours, and, once again uncomfortably wondering where all the fuel was coming from.

    Jacobs was great to work for, but his shop was in Hermosa Beach, and it turned out to be too far from Cardiff to drive there every day. I was just about ready to open my own shop when I went to work shaping for Hobie in Dana Point. I told him I would work for him for a while before I went on my own.

SURF BIZ

I was living in Del Mar again, this time with a family and a house to live in. When I told my old friend Bob Driver Jr. of my plans to start a surfboard business, he said his dad might loan me whatever money I needed. Mister Driver owned a big insurance company in San Diego. He had helped many young people get started in business.

I had been operating out of somebody's garage when I approached Mister Driver. He asked me how much I needed to get started. I didn't know anything about business, so I just threw some figure out there, fifteen hundred dollars. Driver said he'd put up the 1,500 and that I could either take him as a partner and just pay $750 of it back or that I could be my own boss and pay back the entire amount. I thought about it for a day or two and realized that he had all kinds of knowledge that I didn't. It turns out that was the best thing I ever did in business. If that hadn't happened, Op Swimwear might never have occurred. I've saved that story for a later chapter.

HANSEN

Mister Driver was a silent partner, and he was just that—pretty much silent except when I needed his advice. We never had an argument until I decided to buy him out. We were dear friends until he died, and I actually spoke at his funeral. We had a lot of fun together, even though he was 25-years older than me and a really devout Mormon. He gave me advice about being conservative and not overextending myself. He not only gave me good advice, but he had the credit we needed to start buying property. We remained partners for 12 years, until 1973.

Surfing is now about 70 percent of our business, and skiing about 30 percent. But we're far more than a surf shop. One of the main reasons I survived all these years is that I bought all this property around here. I could expand without paying rent. This place would cost me around 50 thousand a month if I had to rent it! But I bought it, and it's all paid for. I never had a backup plan; I just kept putting one foot in front of the other and tell-

SURF BIZ

ing myself this has to work. I'm not sure what I would have done if it didn't.

The business began to turn around sometime in the middle '70s, where we'd sell ski equipment in the winter, and the rest of the time, it would be surf. I barely made any money for years. I got divorced in 1971.

In the early years, I did everything myself. I managed the floor and did all the buying. I think it's essential for the store-owner to know how it all works and know their employees. I still go down to the floor. I don't sell, but I talk to people, and that's all it takes is talking to people and getting to know them. I know that if retail doesn't give good customer service and have friendly, smiling employees, they just aren't going to survive. I felt that one advantage we had over some of the other shapers and guys who were building surfboards was that I grew up with such a strong work ethic.

I started making quite a few boards under the Hansen label but was still driving to Dana Point to shape for Hobie. I'd shape there all day and come back to Cardiff working in a building where a bar named the Kraken now stands. I'd build boards there until morning. I shaped, sanded, hot coated, glossed, and rubbed out. I also put the fins on, but I think I got fins from someone else and then sanded them down a little. I'd be working there until three or four in the morning with dust flying around all over the place. Hardly anyone ever wore a mask in those days, and I attribute shaping and sanding without a mask to the asthma I have today. Eventually, I became allergic to foam dust. Even now, I'll walk into a shaping room and start sneezing. I didn't fall in love with shaping the way some guys do, and asthma was just one of the things that convinced me that I didn't want to be a shaper all my life.

There was a restaurant/bar across the street from our first shop in Cardiff called "George's." It's where the Chart House is now, and a man named George San Clemente owned it. One day Greg Noll came to the shop, and we went across the street to George's to eat and maybe have a few beers. We were at the bar when Greg decided it was a good idea to piss into a cup. George didn't like that very much. [Laughs hard]

While Don had many wild times, he never shirked his responsibilities. He managed the delicate balance between fun, sports, and the family he loves. Heidi Garvey Hansen is the only Hansen daughter. She was just a child growing up as the lone female in a tribe of triple-plus Alpha males. This has contributed to her being courageous, compassionate, and good at business.

According to Heidi:

I missed him terribly when I was a kid after the divorce, and I was scared all the time without him. My mom finally dropped us off at his house one morning because she could not care for us as she was going thru so much pain. Dad did all he could for us. He did a great job, and he wanted us from the beginning. I love him for that. He went from being a very popular and good-looking 38-year-old bachelor to being a single father of three kids: a five-year-old, a nine-year-old, and a 13-year-old. My older brothers stayed with my mom.

Seeing my father walk through the door was like seeing God. He was such a big hero to me. When I was really young, he wasn't around a lot because he worked so much. Still, he made sure we were all well taken care of. When I was about nine years old, he was doing a lot of skydiving. I tried skydiving tandem with the boys. I was really into athletics, but the men in my family are such adrenaline junkies it can be hard keeping up.

Don had pretty much stopped surfing when I was young, and just as he does now, he was always looking for the next thing. He never told me all the things he had done, and I just recently learned about things like him living in his car.

It's hard to follow in his footsteps—It's impossible. He's brilliant and kind, and he's taken care of a lot of different people. He built his business when he was a single father.

When I was around 12-years-old, he married Shirley. She is a great stepmother, but she was young when she came in to take over working in the store and raising us kids.

My parents wanted all of us to work somewhere else before we worked at the store. Still, we all learned the retail business and have worked hard to maintain Hansen's at the level it has always been. But it was never all about work, and when it was time to play, we did so as a family. There were many road trips when we were kids listening to *Crosby Stills & Nash* and James Taylor. We did a lot of backpacking in the Sierras. We would drive to Lone Pine, get into a tiny single-engine plane, get flown into some remote region, and be dropped off for days. It was hard work, and we were young. It was like *Survivor*.

We have such an incredible father-daughter relationship. I am so lucky to be able to ride horses every summer and ski with him every winter. He is such a star; I can't believe it. He has instilled such a work ethic in me that I feel guilty if I'm sick and cannot make it to work. It is these years I cherish most. Laughing and playing. He is making up for all those long hours he used to work when I was young. I'll take it all in now. I will ALWAYS be here for him.

My son Jack is 17, and my daughter Makena is 19. Makena recently said this about her grandfather: "My grandpa Don or as I call him "Bumpa" is one of the funniest people I have ever known. He can never hear me correctly, and he's always calling me the wrong name, but it's what I love most about him. He doesn't take himself too seriously, and he really cares about you. His family has always been his number one priority, and I will always admire him for that. It's hard to put into words how inspired I am and how thankful I am to have a grandpa like him." Jack surfs a lot and has carried on the family's surf legacy in that way even more than my brothers have.

As a family, we've been through a lot, and the things I learned from my dad have really helped. He always taught us that no

> matter what, life goes on. There's been a lot of hardship, but there's also a lot of affection in our family—A lot of hugging and kissing. I cry tears of joy, thinking he is my father.

Hansen Surfboards

I had three kids and a wife when Hobie fired me. Still, I wasn't worried about surviving since surfing was taking off in the Encinitas area, and I was already making enough surfboards on my own. I had only worked for Hobie a few months when I realized I would have to quit to keep up with all my own orders. I was ready to turn in my resignation when Hobie surprised me and beat me to it. I think he had found out how many boards I was making and didn't want the competition. He didn't remember firing me, but I said, "Bullshit, Hobie, you *did* fire me!" Years later, we would laugh about that. Thirty years after he let me go, we became good friends and business partners when I sold him some of my shares in Ocean pacific (Op.)

Hobie and I ran our businesses similarly—we were both pretty conservative in business. Still, he was different from me because he was more of a tinker than I ever was. Other than that, we both followed more of an established line toward success in the surfboard business. I was doing something that had been done before. Hobie was too, but he was like Doyle in a way— an out on the edge type thinker. Hobie went from one thing to another—from surfboards to catamarans, to model airplanes and kayaks. He really did a lot.

Besides being fired by Hobie, the only other time I got fired from a job was back when I was in high school in South Dakota. Actually, I quit that job. The man's name was Frank Christian, and every kid who ever worked for him left after a week or two. He was impossible to work for and just so hard on everyone. The building we were working on at the time is still in Redfield. It's a Quonset hut type building, and my job was to put shingles on it.

It was really windy one day, and I almost got blown off the ladder a couple times.

SURF BIZ

Frank had gone somewhere to do something else. While he was gone, I began cutting the bundles of shingles in half to carry 50 pounds up the ladder rather than 100. I wasn't being lazy; I was simply trying to stay alive. When Frank returned, he got really pissed at me and yelled, "What the hell are you doing cutting those things in half; you can carry up the whole bundle one at a time." I had already outlasted all the other guys by being there for three weeks. After listening to his lecture, I finally said, "You know what, Frank, I quit too." I turned around, walked away, and went to work on a farm somewhere.

By 1963 I was well enough established in the surfboard industry to hire more glassers, glossers, sanders, and shapers. We only had three or four employees when we started. They were great craftsmen, and Templin brothers and the Brummett brothers were among them. There were two or three old local families that worked for us, and I never had many problems finding good workers. Ron Smith, one of the guys who started the

Chart House, worked to manage my factory in Solana Beach for two years.

I barely paid myself a salary for several years. One of those shapers was John Price. I think he learned to shape at Hansen's. Not long after learning to shape, he took a week off to go to Hawaii. Upon his return, he told me that he had bought Surfboards Hawaii and was going to open up his own shop in Encinitas. It pissed me off, and I told him so. He said, "You can't afford to fire me; I'm the only shaper you've got right now." I said, "Okay, let me think about this." I thought about it overnight, came back the next morning, and fired him. Eventually, over the years, we became friends again. I can't hold a grudge; you just destroy yourself.

In a way, what Price had done wasn't much different from what I had done with Hobie. The big difference was that I told Hobie I had planned on opening up a surfboard shop of my own from the time I began working with him.

SURF BIZ

As anyone in the surfboard business will tell you, the minute the surf comes up, everyone's gonna be at least two or three hours late for work. They come in with their hair wet and ready to work, which was all right by me. It's just something you had to put up with if you wanted to be in the surfboard business. It wasn't like we were swamped with business initially anyway, and I was still surfing quite a bit myself in those years. So it really didn't bother me when they showed up late. Plus, I had a good crew, and they always got their work done.

    One thing I regret is not keeping the name Cardiff somewhere on our company logo. Cardiff-By-The-Sea; what a great name, especially before everybody had heard of it. It was in there on our logo when our shop was located in Cardiff, but... I don't really tell many people this, but I always figured we helped put Cardiff-By-The Sea on the map. It wasn't well known beyond San Diego proper before the '70s.

While the surfboard business was never very lucrative, eventually, I made enough money to buy a house. We bought our first house up on the hill in Del Mar for $22,000. It was a beautiful home with a view of the surf. When I sold it a while later for $40,000, we thought we were rich. I hate to think what it would sell for now.

I was never that competitive in surfing, but I managed to get first or second in an East Coast surf contest once. I was still surfing by the mid-'60s, but not nearly as often as I once had. Still, I managed to win the U.S. Championships at Huntington Beach in the tandem event with Diane Bolton around that time, and I took second place in tandem at Makaha. When the trophies got rusted up, I just tossed them.

By 1967 the surfboard business was profitable. We moved out of our first retail store/factory in Cardiff to our current location at 1105 South Coast Highway 101, Encinitas. When they remodeled the building we had been in to make way for a fun little bar

SURF BIZ

known as the Kraken, they found all kinds of Hansen memorabilia stuffed into the walls. Some of the guys brought in price sheets and other items to me, and it was amazing to see that double-glassed custom surfboards were a little more than a hundred dollars at the time. I can't imagine what it would cost to build something like that now.

Over the last few years, we've had a lot of great shapers make our boards. John Price, George Lanning, Duane Brown, Willy Clark, Richard Templin, Mike Doyle, Mike Holidick, Jim Hovde, Bill Thrailkill, and Craig Hollingsworth are among them.

In 1967 there was nothing but a couple of little sheds at 1105 S. Highway 101 in Encinitas, where our store now stands. The only thing I could think to do was turn the place into a diverse retail store since, in 1969, the surfboard business was going to hell.

One of our properties at our new location was an old gas station on Coast Highway. There's a pipe that goes under the property there, and EPA found a gas leak. It wasn't much of a leak really and didn't cause any real harm to the environment, but in the end, it cost us thirty years and three-quarters of a million dollars to clean it all up. We got about half a million of it back through insurance, but still... Nobody realized at the time what the potential liability was for pollution. It's ridiculous what they make you do. We figured that they might have lost four or five hundred gallons of fuel through leakage over 50 years! Nothing was coming up under the ground; nobody smelled anything. None of the people near our store cared; they were all really cooperative. Still, we monitored the cliffs for thirty-some years.

I asked the lady running the health department in San Diego for the county what she majored in at school. I figured it would be something to do with the environment, but she said, "Oriental Literature!" I told her, "Mam, we did not cause the pollution on the property, so why do we have to clean it up?" She looked at me and smiled and said, "We don't care who caused it; you own it now, and you're gonna

SURF BIZ

pay for it!" I can't see where they've done one bit of good. That's one reason I got out of the surfboard business because I knew they were going to shut 'em all down. The big thing now is methane. The EPA wants things cleaner than what they would be in nature. We had to put a vacuum system under the ground for two or three years before they told us we didn't need to do that anymore. Most military and government sites do nothing to clean up their areas, claiming they don't have the money to clean them up. Somehow though they think small businesses do have that kind of money,

By 1969 I could see that building boards by hand was no longer going to be profitable. That's when we had the first shaping machine built. The machine copied the exact shape of a surfboard using a router. It was kind of my idea, but I'm not a machinist, and I give all the credit to Don Oakey, a surfer from La Jolla. Don was the one who designed and built the shaping machine, and it became the forerunner for all the machines that are in use now. He was a genius and great fun to work with.

HANSEN

We tried many different things, from blowing our own blanks to making Strata glass-molded surfboards to stay in the surfboard manufacturing business. In 1971 we were the first ones I'm aware of to make hollow surfboards. To make them, I copied the method Hobie used on his catamarans. It's a sandwich process, molding both halves separately. They had a hole in the nose to drain them, and we ended up using the plugs from squirt guns as a seal. We must have had 500 squirt guns lying around without any plugs. [Laughs] The big problem we had with them was bonding them together. We guaranteed them, and we probably replaced about 50 percent of them over the years. Eventually, we realized that some people were standing on them to break the seal so they could get a new board. Still, we took care of everyone who brought their boards back. By the early '70s, our board sales plummeted from about 5,000 boards a year down to around 2,500. That occurred in one year, and we knew that

SURF BIZ

if that trend continued, we wouldn't be in the manufacturing business much longer.

I was conservative in business, but I did take some chances. While some of those changes worked, others like the hollow boards we experimented with nearly took us out of business. It looked like the surfboard business was going toward molded boards in the early '70s. Still, it's taken until recently for them to become dominant. We were way ahead on that one, and I still have one of those boards as a memento of a failed enterprise.

After our molded board experiment didn't work, I needed some quick cash and had to sell my collection of classic surfboards. I had a Simmons, a couple of kook boxes, and a Hot Curl that I sold for $1,500. What really hurt the surfboard market was when boards went short in the mid-'60s, and guys began stripping the glass from old longboards for the blanks. In time many of those garage guys learned the craft and went into business for themselves. In the long run, that's the way industries work.

HANSEN

We tried everything we could think of to survive, including making surf skis. One design we called "The Shoe" was pretty popular. Mike Johnson got me interested in surf skis, and he taught me to ride them. I got to where I could do the Eskimo Roll and a 360 down the face of the wave on them. They were a lot of fun, and I wish I still had one of them.

We explored a lot of different avenues in manufacturing and in the retail store where we carried tennis gear and backpacking equipment. We became a general sporting goods store for a while. Still, eventually, surfboards, skis, and snowboards remained at the core of our business. We've never quit selling surfboards, but there were times when we weren't carrying many of them. Now we have over 400 surfboards from various manufactures on hand. Once we realized that skiing and surfing were our mainstays, we remodeled the store around them.

I'm getting ahead of myself here, but in April of 2003, I was in Hawaii for Dave Rochlin's

SURF BIZ

funeral. Rochlin was such a character. Who else do you know who organized his own funeral right down to the smallest detail? He owned a company called Surfline that he bought from its founder, Dick Metz. Rochlin also started the famous boardshort company, Jams. The name Jams was short for pajamas, which is how those trunks were initially made.

Dick Metz has been involved in the surfing industry since its inception. He had this to say about Rochlin, Hobie, and his meeting Don Hansen.

> Dave Rochlin's wife Kanui sewed the first pairs of Jams in their living room from a pair of pajamas. That's where the name Jams came from [pa Jam as.] I ran the Hobie store in Honolulu, and we began Jams once they had more than a few pairs. When the Hobie team came to Makaha from the Mainland, I put Jams on all of them, which caused the brand to soar.

> Initially, the Hobie shop carried only Hobie Surfboards. When I saw the need to carry other lines and started Surfline in Hawaii. We had a variety of surfboards. I put ten boards from various manufacturers in Surfline. I had known Don from my time running Hobie in Dana Point and carried 10 of his boards. That began a lifelong friendship between Don and me. Once we both got into skiing, Don and I and our wives would go to different ski resorts together for a month at a time.

They still make Jams and Rochlin's son, Dave Pua Rochlin, runs the company. During Dave Sr's memorial, we were on two big catamarans a few miles off Waikiki. They let a flock of pigeons go at the ceremony, and instead of heading for land, the birds flew out to sea. [Laughs] After the ceremony, legendary surfer/board maker Joe Quigg approached me, saying he had always wanted to meet me. He was interested in knowing how I had adapted Hobie's idea of molding catamarans into surfboard manufacturing. I was shocked

SURF BIZ

that an innovator like Quigg would be interested in what I was doing. That was the only time I ever met him.

Before Freeway Five was completed in the late 1960s, we would duck hunt in Cardiff's San Elijo Lagoon. We would then sit on an onramp near the bridge and pick off a few ducks for dinner.

    On the beachside of the lagoon near Cardiff Reef, I started making and selling surfboards in Cardiff. As I mentioned, the building is now called the Kraken and is a popular bar in town. Local fisherman Stan Lewis would stop by my shop after he finished fishing, at around 11 a.m. He always had a bottle of something in his back pocket. He would offer me a drink, but I was in the middle of my workday, so I don't think I ever took him up on it. Stan was something, though. He was a fantastic waterman, and I'd watch him drive back and forth in the shallows in his fishing skiff, waiting until he saw a lull in the waves, and there was a chance of getting out. Then I'd see him racing to get over that last wave, and his boat would leave the water after squeaking over the top. He knew exactly what he was doing and eventually taught his son, Tommy, everything he knew. Tommy became an outstanding local surfer, shaper, and fisherman himself.

Stan once tried to sell me his house up on the hill at Cardiff. He said, "Someday, you'll be sitting up here, and you'll see a three-masted schooner come into the harbor. " The state was planning on building a series of marinas up and down the coast at the time, and Cardiff was selected as one of them before the whole idea was scrapped.

Ocean Pacific

"I'd rather be with my worst enemy in the surfboard business than my best friend in the clothing company."
-Greg Noll

I bought the name Ocean pacific from John Smith in 1971 for $1,500. That's the same amount I initially used to start our surfboard business a decade earlier. Jim Jenks had

SURF BIZ

come up with the idea of creating a clothing company. Through my business, California Surfing Products, he learned about clothing. Our surfboard company was on the edge of going broke, so I invested along with Jenks, Chuck Butler, and Bob Driver. After Hobie sold his Hobie Cat business, [Dick] Metz convinced him into buying some of my shares of Ocean pacific. Thirty years after he fired me, Hobie and I became good friends and business partners.

After around 12 years in the clothing business, my partners decided to sell Op. It turned out that I had never legally signed the name over to them. It wasn't really a temptation to sell the name to them for a lot of money, but... I turned it over to them for nothing.

A lot of the guys in the surfboard business can trace their ancestry back to us. Among them is John Price, who owned the Surfboards Hawaii label in California; Mike Doyle and Rusty Miller, who founded Surf Research [which later became Wax Research] and Jim Jenks, the first CEO of Ocean pacific.

HANSEN

Duke Boyd had Hang Ten, and he was really the first one to crack the surfboard industry with surf clothing. When we started Op, things were kind of rough for Hang Ten, and we kind of took over the market at that time. By the mid-'70s, half the kids in the country had those corduroy Op walk shorts. I think we launched the company for $50,000. I didn't have enough money, and Jim Jenks and our other partner Chuck Butler didn't have much of anything. Mister Driver said he would borrow the money from the bank but that I would have to put my name on the loan with him because I had a few assets. Bob wasn't a surfer, but indirectly he was a significant influence on the entire surfing industry. Without clothing and T-shirts and all that, the surfing industry never would have survived.

When we first moved into our current location, we used the back rooms for shipping and storing, and we ever rubbed out some rails and things like that back there. I still have guys come in all the time and tell me

SURF BIZ

they rubbed out rails in that back room. We shipped the first half-million dollars worth of Op goods from there in its first year.

Jim Jenks first envisioned Ocean pacific in the early '70s. Among his other accomplishments is starting the Stone Steps Contest, where each participant had to drink a resin bucket of beer before each heat. Jim fondly recalls his days working for and with Don Hansen. According to Jenks:

From Imperial Beach to Dana Point and beyond, every area had its own board builder. Hansen was well established when Surfboards Hawaii, Sunset Surfboards, Channin, and others got going in Encinitas. Don went out of his way to be sure it was good for everybody. He and all the other manufacturers in the area would work together, lending labor back and forth or borrowing a drum of resin or other supplies when needed.

Don allowed me to do a lot of things that not many other employers would have. He let me run California Surfing Products, which eventually became Ocean pacific, out of his shop.

Before we launched Op, some of us would drive up from San Diego to Katin's in Orange County to get a pair of trunks made from sailcloth by Nancy Katin. They were great, but they were stiff as a board, and if you lived in trunks like most of us did at the time, you ended up getting the rash from hell. [Laughs] That was a big inspiration in starting Op, making trunks that wouldn't give you a rash.

I began working for Don in the early '60s. He enjoyed the production end of it, and I liked sales. I'd take California Surfing Products, which consisted of Hansen Surfboards, wetsuits, a bikini line, surf wax, Surfer Magazine products, and other surf-related accessories to the East Coast. I'd leave Cardiff right after the Super Bowl and end up in Ogunquit, Maine. Somewhere along the line, I decided the world needed surfing trunks.

I didn't have any real money and asked Don to help me launch the line. He asked me to meet with him and his business partner, Bob Driver, and they ended up backing me. I was still running Don's showroom at the time and working as a traveling rep.

I was doing my rounds on the East Coast and was leaving a surf shop when a guy approached me and said, "If I ever got out to California, I would sure like to work in a surfboard factory." I was on my way out the door with my order in my hand when I said, 'Come by and ask for Jim and I'll get you set up in the factory.' I didn't think any more about it, but a month later, I arrived at work, and this guy was sitting out in the parking lot, asleep in this old Volkswagen. I woke him to say we were about to open soon. I didn't remember him, but he opened his eyes and said, "Hey, Jim, remember me?" It was the guy I had promised a job to, and he was there for a job I didn't have for him. I excused myself, walked up to Don, and said, 'Hey, Don, I've got a problem; I kind of told this guy I'd give him a job.' He said, "That's okay, take him down to the factory, and I'll call down and tell them he's coming." Don called up and said, "A guy is coming down looking for work; find something for him." He gave the guy a job without ever having met him or knowing what he could do. That's how Don is about everything and everybody. He always goes the extra mile, and if he says he will do something, he'll definitely do it. He was such an honorable guy. I could not have had a better partner than Don Hansen.

Once Op really got going, we had to separate. Don and I shook hands, and I rented the building he owned across the street from Hansen Surfboards. Don knew what surfing clothing could be and that surfboards could only go so far.

Hansen Surfboards was starting to do well, and as we began getting known, I began meeting some interesting characters. Greg Noll, Pat Curren, and Mike Doyle are all legendary. Each of them has insane stories in the surfing world, but Jack "Murf the Surf" was legendary for things beyond just surfing. Murf was

SURF BIZ

the first East Coast Surfing champion, and I met him one evening through George Draper over dinner at the Chart House in Shelter Island. Soon after that, Murf was caught stealing the Star of India, the world's largest star sapphire, and 22 other precious gems from the J.P. Morgan collection at the American Museum of Natural History. Later, Murf was accused of murder, but George knew him well and said there was no way he was a murderer. Murf was a fascinating character. I only met him that once, and maybe that was enough.

A friend from my childhood in Redfield, Wesley Grapp, later joined the FBI and rose in the ranks until he was in charge of the department's Los Angeles division. He had lived next door to my parents in Mansfield, South Dakota, and had once worked on our family's farm. My mom and dad became like surrogate parents to him because he had a tough old dad that he never got along very well with.

Years later, when my parents came out to see me in Cardiff, they would drive up to L.A. and see Wesley and take him out to dinner. I was learning to fly at the time, and my dad and I took an old twin-engine Apache to L.A. to visit Wesley. Those planes were underpowered, and I recall feeling that they could barely get off the ground.

Anyway, this was right after Murf got arrested, and we were talking about his capture over dinner. When I told Wesley that I once had dinner with Murf the Surf, he looked at me like I was some sort of criminal myself. Talk about a small world—the FBI had traced Murf through a watermark on some dry cleaning he left in L.A. It turns out that Wesley himself was intimately involved in capturing Murphy. It was a remarkable coincidence. I tried to explain to him that I was just a surfer and didn't really know Murf very well at all, but Wesley never really trusted me after that.

Misadventures in Sailing

Ever since I was a kid, I've looked for new adventures. Sailing seemed like a natural extension to surfing, so I bought a Woody

SURF BIZ

Brown designed catamaran with an asymmetrical hull. I think Woody designed catamarans even before Hobie began making them. One year some friends and I decided to enter the Newport to Ensenada International Sailboat Race. It was always held in May, and after we started the race in Newport, the wind came up, really hard. By that afternoon, it was blowing 25 to 30 miles per hour, and we were just whistling down the coast. Onboard with me were my factory manager Ron Smith and my friend, George Draper. I think the reason we survived that trip was that Wayne Shaffer came along at the last minute. He was the only one of us with any ocean racing experience. We did okay for a while, but we needed all the assistance we could get once it got dark, even with his help. I knew how to sail and had been aboard boats a lot, but we probably would have all drowned without Shaffer. He wasn't a big surfer, but he knew a lot about sailing. He was a good friend, and he just died recently. Since we were racing and wanted to make good time, we threw everything we could think overboard, including the anchor.

    We whistled into Ensenada the next day around noon, and a lot of the boats, including one called the *Morning Star*, which set a record that year, had already been there for hours. Phil Edwards, whom I considered the best surfer in the world at one time, was in that race on his cat, *El Gato*. I think legendary surfer Mickey Munoz was part of his crew. They made it in like twelve hours and had been in port for a while. While everyone else was in partying, we were still out there, floundering offshore all night. I didn't realize how far offshore we were, but we were three, four, five miles west of them when we passed the Coronado Islands. It was nearly dark by then, and we couldn't see them at all. The wind was still blowing hard when we made Ensenada Harbor. A few ships were coming in while we tried to figure out how to stop our boat without an anchor. We whistled by somebody on a boat we knew, and even though we had our mainsail way down, we were still going way too

SURF BIZ

fast to pull into a slip. We hollered at someone on a boat that we were going to come by one more time, and when we did, we were going to throw them a line. Someone shouted, "Hang on because we need to get stopped so we can get moored somewhere." By the time we got moored, we had finished in like 20 hours. We had no idea what we were doing.

We deiced to use our Johnson outboard motor on the way back. We were heading into the wind and got about 20 miles up the coast from Ensenada, figuring we would be back in San Diego by that afternoon. But we were tired of it all by then and decided to run that sucker up onto the beach, leave it there and come back for it later. We found a good beach to get upon, where a guy was driving a Caterpillar, doing some work on the beach. I gave the guy 50 bucks to take the Caterpillar and pull the catamaran up another hundred yards or so. We just left it there, and about one week later, I hired a big truck and drove down with John Price and someone else. I don't know how we got that thing onto the truck, but we somehow managed it before driving back up the highway to home. I didn't sail much after that.

Shortboards, Shaping Machines and Hollow Boards

Overnight surfboards had gone from ten feet to around seven feet. That changed the whole industry and the way everyone surfed. Within a year, you couldn't find a noserider or any type of longboard for sale in any shop, and just like that, nearly was on shortboards. Some of the best boards ever made were virtually worthless then, as people stripped them of their glass and cut down the blank. Only a few guys rode longboards at that time, and I believe Phil Edwards was one of them. Phil wasn't surfing much by then; he was more into sailing. Never a contest surfer or someone trying to get his photo in the magazines, Phil was pretty much forgotten by most surfers then. Before that, however, he was the best surfer I had ever seen. He rode a longboard with unmatched style like it was a magic carpet. He could do anything on a surf-

SURF BIZ

board. Same with John Peck. John rode for us for a while. John was also an unbelievable surfer, and he did get into shortboards. They worked well with his on-edge style of surfing, which revolved around tube riding and radical turns.

Just before boards went short, Hobie, Bing, Jacobs, and I all bought our blanks from Grubby (Clark.) It was Hobie who got him started in the business. During the transition from longboards to shortboards in the late '60s, many guys who had never previously made surfboards began figuring it out by building them in their parent's garages.

As I mentioned, at first, the backyard guys simply peeled the glass from their old boards, reshaped the blanks, and glassed them in their parent's garages. That movement cut into our sales significantly. When sales dropped another 25 percent the following year, I started phasing out of manufacturing. We still retained a shaping room but began taking boards elsewhere to get glassed. There's never been a lot of money made in manufacturing surfboards anyway. One of the only ones that made real money was Grubby Clark because everybody needs blanks. Hobie made money, but he was always into other things like I was. I started switching my retail operation over from just surfing around 1971. We got into skateboarding, backpacking, tennis, and skiing. Eventually, we reduced it down to surfing, beach equipment, skiing, and snowboarding.

Dan's oldest son, Christian, has been a big part of the Encinitas surf scene since his youth. He has followed the family tradition into other adrenaline-driven sports like skiing and skydiving. Christian had the following to say about his upbringing:

Growing up in Encinitas was really cool. The Swami's crew took me under their wing from an early age. I would come in from surfing and play volleyball at the foot of the stairs. At the time, I was a dishwasher at the Sandwich Hutt, across from our store. I was 14-years-old, and once the last dish was washed, I would run down to Swami's with my board and dive in. I think I traded that board for some beers. The next day I saw the kid who had owned the board cruising the lot with his father driving him around in his BMW. I swear he looked right at me but didn't point me out to his dad. I was scared shitless, but I think he was even more scared because he never did come to Swami's again. We were kind of the Bad Co Boys, and a lot of what we did is not suitable for print.

In the mid-'80s, I went to work for John Bernard. I can't say enough about what a great guy he was, and he made me Offshore Sportswear regional rep. I had the time of my life, surfing, skiing, and skydiving.

Everyone has his or her own path, but I look up to my dad. He is definitely someone to look up to, and this makes me strive to do more. He is strict, honest, humble, and straightforward. No B.S., even though I know, I wasn't the easiest kid to raise.

In 1979, when I was 17-years-old, I drove my Baja bug to Mammoth and met my dad there. He took me heli-skiing along with Randy Stits, Mike Lewis, and Rusty Gregory, who eventually became the CEO of Mammoth Mountain. It had snowed six feet in three days and the pilot, who had his hair in a ponytail, looked to me like he was really stoned. He said he had been a Medevac pilot in Viet Nam and that flying a helicopter was like driving a car for him. He drove the chopper straight down a valley at 120 knots... Yeeew! That was a day to remember, and there were many others.

Once, my dad and I made a father/son trip to a remote part of Alaska. We fly fished for giant rainbow trout and King Salmon. Our mode of transportation was the De Havalin Beaver that we landed on small lakes and rivers. Some of those landings were super dicey!

When I was a little kid, we often went to the Driver's beach house in Del Mar. One day my dad took me out on his board with him and let me stand up while he hung onto me. Eventually, he began pushing me into waves, and the rest came with practice. There were no boards for groms back then, so he had built me a four-foot Hansen 50/50 model for the WindanSea Menehune Contests. I loved the surf contests, and I remember being around five or six-years-old, being cold and wet in my singlet, and waiting for my dad to say that everything was okay.

 I was around ten-years-old when I brought the "Masters of the Sky" video to my fifth-grade class taught by Mister Walker. My dad was really into skydiving by then, and he loaned me the movie. Everyone was mesmerized, and Mister Walker ended up doing a static line jump two weeks later.

 Over the next two years, my dad won two National Championships in the Speed Star event. He captained that team, and they broke several world records in formation skydiving.

 By the time I was 18, he had retired from that sport, but I still had the bug. It was a family thing with brother Josh and my sister Heidi who has done four tandem jumps. The feeling of skydiving is unexplainable. There is nothing like flying up to a family member in free fall. You've heard the saying, "Only a surfer knows the feeling?" Just plug in the word "skydiver," and you'll understand.

I feel both blessed and proud to be in this business with my brother and sister. The love I feel from them, and the entire community is worth everything. Whenever someone approaches me to say how much they love coming into our store, my eyes beam with pride. This store will be here long after I'm gone.

Some of my dad's rules:

1) Don't ever be late for work.

2) Don't ever call in sick when you have a hangover.

3) Most important to him: Find something you love doing and try to make a living at it.

As I've gotten older, I realize that I've been very fortunate in my business opportunities.

SURF BIZ

Because of that, I try to spread it around a little. I like to support charities, especially those benefitting ex-military, children, and animals. Over the years, we have given scholarships to five or six different schools every year.

I'm glad we're able to do that, and one of the reasons we can is because we've been conservative in business and didn't open up a chain of stores. People often ask me why we still only have one store, but I'm glad we did it that way. It used to be that when someone was opening a new mall, they would call to see if I wanted to open a new store. I had seen many guys in the ski and surf business open shops all over, but around 95 percent of them went bankrupt. I had the philosophy early on that I didn't want to live to work; I wanted to work to live. I knew that we'd have difficulty finding people to run them if we had five or six stores.

The one store we have now covers around 25,000 square feet, and about 17,000 of that is retail. For years after we opened, the entrance in the front. We had a really old anchor sitting out front until some bastard stole the thing one night. But we're always remodeling our store. We've had two major addition projects since opening until now, we're nearly out of property.

In hiring employees, I would take someone with common sense over someone with a college education in a minute. Of course, the best is if they have both common sense and a solid education. But you can't teach common sense—people either have it, or they don't.

Even with good employees, they claim 75 percent of theft in stores is from employees. While I don't think ours is that high, we've had our share. We once caught a kid who was a customer stealing a wetsuit. You could see the collar sticking out above his shirt. He was so personable, however, that when we confronted him, we ended up hiring him. One of the kids I caught stealing from us was the son of a mayor in Del Mar. We were always pretty lenient with them unless they were robbing us blind. If we ever call the cops on

SURF BIZ

the kids, they let us handle it. We usually turn it over to their parents, and I let them take it from there. I think most of the kids wished we had the cops handle it rather than face their dads. [Laughs]

The East Coast of the U.S. was a big market for surfboards, and we would drive out there regularly to promote our newest models. When we did that, we always brought along some of the talented members of our surf team. Two of the best were our team riders John Peck and Linda Benson.

Coming through the south in those days, you had to watch what you did and said cuz these southern boys didn't like people coming in from the north interfering with their politics. Peck had a little camera with him when we traveled, and he kept getting out of the car whenever we stopped to take pictures of these "White Only" signs at gas stations. I mean, none of us could believe seeing that, but I had to tell him to put his camera away. He didn't do it until some guy saw John taking a picture, came up to the car, and said, "You boys better get the hell out of here." I did before turning around and saying, "Okay, John, that's it; you're not taking any more pictures of anything."

Linda Benson, who was along on that trip, recalls, "John had a bad cold, and he kept spitting out the window, and it would come back onto the side of the car. Don didn't like that very much."

Don was lifeguarding Moonlight Beach in Encinitas when he first also met Linda. She was barely in her early teens but already showed great promise as a surfer. By her mid-teens, Linda was among the best women surfers in the world, winning the U.S. Championships in Huntington Beach five times. She excelled in Hawaii's big surf and won what was in 1959 the most prestigious surf contest in the world, The Makaha International Surfing Championships.

It was a pleasure sponsoring Linda. She was then, and she remains a really nice

SURF BIZ

person. The other outstanding woman surfer I sponsored was Margo Godfrey. She eventually became Margo Oberg and would win five Women's World Championships. I was Margo's chaperone the first time she went to Hawaii. There was no talk then about her riding for us, but she eventually did so and won her first World Title in Puerto Rico in 1968 on a Hansen Surfboard. She was in her early teens when I first took her to the Islands. A famous young surfer from California who was quite a bit older than Margo was kind of after her. I told him to knock it off because she was only 14. But Linda was the first woman we sponsored.

By the time Hansen Surfboards was established, Benson was invited to join the prestigious Hansen Surf Team. She was one of the first sponsored females in a sport then dominated nearly exclusively by boys and young men. The following are among Linda's memories of her early days as a surfer and her enduring friendship with Don. According to Benson:

I was 11-years-old in the summers of 1954. We grew up within walking distance of Moonlight Beach, and that was where we hung out. We lived in Encinitas, where the population was 5,000, and everyone knew each other. Moonlight Beach had everything: a sidewalk café with a jukebox, a teen center with Ping-Pong tables. There were palm-frond shaded benches where the older people could sit and watch whatever was happening. Surfers John Elwell, Fred Ashley, and Fred Wilkins were among the lifeguards there. They played Hawaiian music over the speakers for all the beach to hear. Wayne Land and some others would shape surfboards behind the lifeguard tower.

 A man named Frank Hipsley had a place to rent surf mats. I worked there renting mats in exchange for a free mat to ride. Julie Foster, who would later marry lifeguard Bill Hunt, and I would ride mats together. We were fearless on them, taking them out on the biggest days and riding in on our knees, putting our hands over our heads after making the drop.

One day, my older brother and his friends were standing around in the backyard, looking at his new surfboard. Before that, I hadn't paid much attention to the five or six surfers who surfed in our area. I followed my brother and his friends to the beach that day and stood on the cliff to watch. That was really the first time I noticed surfing, and I immediately wanted to try it.

After that, I began standing close to shore, in knee- to waist-deep water. There I would retrieve boards when someone lost them. One day someone offered to let me ride his board. It was a ten-foot Simmons, and I paddled out before the surfer spun me around and pushed me into a wave. I didn't weigh very much, and I rode that first wave all the way to shore. I still have the vision stamped in my memory, the water rushing beneath me.

It was like Pandora's box had been opened, and from then on, I hung around the lifeguards and asked to use their boards. They would let me do that, even though I couldn't lift them, and I'd stay out until they came to get me.

One day a surfer who would eventually shape for Hansen, Mike Holidick, offered to sell me his 8'6" waterlogged balsa board made by Buzzy Bent for 20 dollars. My dad wasn't sure about letting me have a surfboard until John Elwell told him that I was a good swimmer and was careful in the ocean. I bought that board, and Wayne Land reshaped it behind the lifeguard tower into a 7'6" pig board with a blue and white abstract on the deck.

That's around the time I met Don Hansen. He was from South Dakota and living in his panel truck, but he became one of the guys right away. By 1963 I was riding for Hansen, and I traveled with Don, his wife, and one of the top surfers of the day, John Peck, on a promotional tour to the East Coast. Flea Shaw was the up-and-coming surfer on the East Coast at the time, and we stayed with him and his family on the beach. We were just kids, but we knew that Don was a good man and that we could always go to him if needed. He did things right, worked hard, had good business sense, and got many good suggestions from his business partner, Bob Driver.

Hansen made me my own skateboard signature model along with a model for L.J. Richards. I worked in the factory, putting roller derby wheels on the boards before sliding them into plastic bags. From there, Don sent me to L.A. to sell them. There were no big sporting goods stores at that time, so I went to the hardware stores. Once there, I'd take out aboard and do a skateboarding demonstration on the sidewalk.

In 1965 I went to work for United Airlines. I was still riding Hansen Surfboards when I was asked to be on a show called "The Wonderful World of Bill Byrd." The camera crew followed me through my airline duties and then over to the Hansen shop. After that, we went to Swami's, where they filmed me surfing.

In the mid-'50s, Rusty Miller [who became the 1965 U.S. Surfing Champion and was one of Hansen's top team riders] had just begun surfing. One day when the surf was big at Moonlight, we couldn't get out, and we sat together on a clump of seaweed crying because of it.

Eventually, Rusty and I started surfing Swami's. I was afraid of the eelgrass, so he would paddle me into the waves, and every time I lost my board, he'd paddle in and get it. Finally, I lost my board and looked at him, but instead of getting my board this time, he just shook his head as if to say, "You're on your own."

Rusty Miller was among the world's top surfers when he moved to Australia in the early 1970s.
According to Miller:

Don was living in his panel truck and surfing Swami's. I would see him around town a lot. When he began making boards, I became his top rider before Mike Doyle moved to town. By the mid-'60s, he financed a company that Doyle, Garth Murphy, and I started called

SURF BIZ

"Surf Research." We made and distributed all sorts of surf-related items from the first custom surf wax [before this surfers melted paraffin wax onto the decks of their boards] to packets of granola. In 1968 we decided to go different ways, and we sold the company to John Baker Dahl. He concentrated strictly on surf and ski wax and renamed the company Wax Research, which is still a thriving business today.

In the mid to late '60s, we had a great shaper working for us named Fred T. Smoles, whom I always called "Buzzard T." for some reason. He was a great craftsman, like Terry Martin, the shaper who worked for Hobie for years. Fred could do anything, and he's such a great guy. He was a good carver and ended up making false teeth for a living. I'd love to hear from him again, but I lost track of him years ago after he moved to McCall, Idaho.

If you're teaching someone to shape surfboards—number one, they have to be a good craftsman. After that, it's what they've got upstairs. Doyle was really good at innovating, and he had great ideas. I learned a lot from Mike, and he taught me to think more outside the box. But I don't think he had ever shaped a surfboard before he started working for us. He began making his Doyle Models for us, and they became a very popular board. He designed and shaped many of them with that square fin of his he called the "pivot fin." We took the gold foil seal from the ones used by notary publics, and used it in his logo.

In the late '60s, I helped fund Surf Research, a company that John Dahl later took over and made into the highly successful Wax Research. But it began with Doyle, Rusty, Garth Murphy, and maybe Fred Ryan. They worked on all sorts of design innovations in a building I owned across the street from our store.

I was raised with such a strong work ethic that it never seemed to me that Doyle and Rusty were working very hard. They were some of the world's top surfers, and I can't really blame them for surfing all the time. Still, one day I walked over and said,

SURF BIZ

"Look, we have a different work ethic; why don't you guys buy me out? I don't remember what they gave me for it, but it wasn't much. I always admired their surfing, and I always liked those guys, and we remained good friends.

Doyle was a great guy, but like all of us, he wasn't completely innocent. Patty Driver once told me that when she and her husband, Bob Jr. were living on Oahu, she had made some pies and left them cooling with the window shutters open. Patty said Doyle came by and stole a couple of them. As far as I know, she never did forgive Mike for that. [Laughs]

But Doyle was definitely a thinker, and when we worked together, I learned a lot from him. He reminded me a little of Jack O'Neill in that way, coming up with all these different ideas. Sometimes he would come to me with a unique vision, and I'd say, "I don't think so, Mike." But at other times, he came up with some excellent ideas like that squared-off fin on his Mike Doyle Model that helped the board pivot into a turn.

HANSEN

A few years before we worked together, I had seen Doyle in Hawaii, where he began making a name for himself in big surf. I lived in one of the plantation shacks in the little cluster of houses near one he had rented the year before. We knew each other then but didn't become good friends until after moving to Leucadia, and we started doing his model for us in the mid-'60s.

The only time I remember being pissed off at him was when he opened his shop *Doyle Sports*, nearly across the street from us. It wasn't unscrupulous, but it always kind of pissed me off. We never did surf together much, and the only surf trip we went on together was when we rented a Cherokee Six airplane, and four of us flew down to Baja. As I recall, the surf wasn't that good, but we had a good time checking out new spots, and he eventually moved down to Baja, where he lived much of his adult life.

Even after Mike moved to Baja, we would get together whenever he came to town. He

SURF BIZ

was one of surfing's all-time water greats and a really nice guy. What else can I say? I always feel the biggest compliment I can give someone is that they were a nice person, and Doyle sure was that. Poor Mike, he died too young. RIP, dear friend. All my love, Annie.

In the late 1960s, Doyle's protégé was a teen-aged surfer from Del Mar named Cheer Critchlow. Cheer, who was among the best surfers ever to come out of the San Diego area, had this to say about Hansen:

Hansen was such a great guy, such a bitchen guy to everyone. On Christmas Day, when I was 14-years-old, living at 15th Street in Del Mar at my parent's house, Don knocked on the door and personally delivered my first board to me. I was so stoked!

Sioux, the woman who would eventually become Cheer's wife, worked the sales floor at Hansen's for several years. Sioux's job interview was unique. According to Sioux:

HANSEN

I was working across the street from Hansen's at a sandwich shop called "The Hutt." Don and his friends, including former Cleveland Browns' quarterback Brian Sipe, came in and ordered some tall beers. When I came to serve the guys, I ended up spilling the beers all over Don's lap. He said, "You're not a very good waitress, but you're a great person, and I'd like to hire you."

The most challenging, hair-raising thing Don asked any of us to do in the shop was help him pack his parachute! We'd never say no, but this was not part of our job descriptions. His chute always opened, but there was a sobering time when Don lost a friend whose chute did not open.

Don was recently honored for his contributions to surfing at the California Surf Museum. He has excelled in so many different things, and in my book, Don Hansen is the John Wayne of the surf community.

Ken Rodgers has worked at Hansen's since May 1993. According to Rodgers:

SURF BIZ

> For the past four years, Don and I have driven from Montana to San Diego together. The trip takes two full days. We get to talk about everything: politics, sports, business, and our family histories. So, I know him pretty well, and I admire his ethics. I recall once when he bought some ski clothing for the store from a competitor in Los Angeles. He hadn't paid for anything, but the buyer didn't realize that. Many owners would have tried playing dumb in order not to pay at all. Not Don. He called to apologize and say the check was on its way, which of course, it was.

Julie King is an avid skier and has been a buyer at Hansen's since 1976. According to Julie:

> I thought about leaving Hansen's once when I went to Steamboat Springs for three weeks to ski. However, while I was there, I could not wait to return to the beach and to Hansen's. Over the years, I've realized that Don is the kindest, most thoughtful person who

always treats his employees with respect and encouragement. Since he treats us all like family, we all feel comfortable going to him for everything. When I bought a house, Don was there to help me with my down payment. One summer, he sent La and me to Europe as thanks for our many years at Hansen's. In return, if he needs help with anything, we are always there for him. Every day at Hansen's creates a new memory because Don has so many great stories to tell and always keeps us laughing. I wasn't surprised that Don paid us when the shop closed after Covid hit. That's who he is. He would give you the shirt off his back.

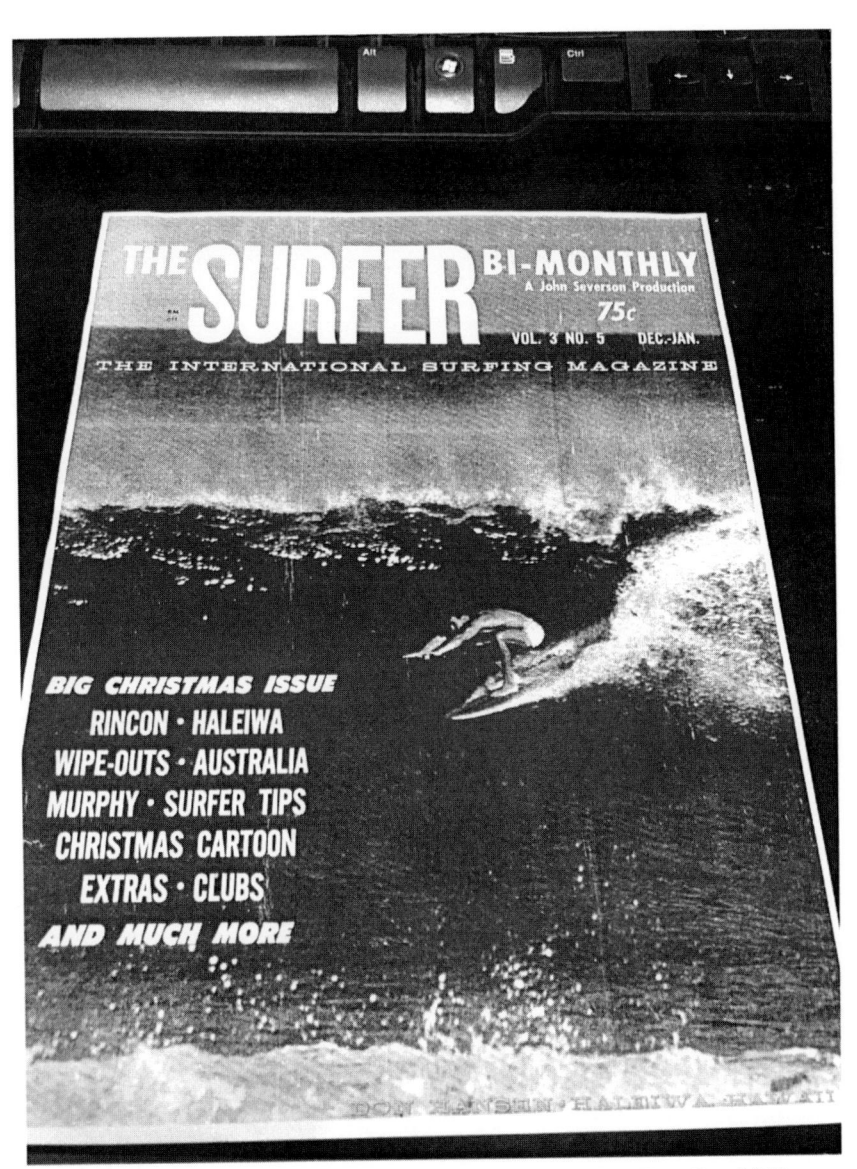

Don Hansen. Cover Surfer Magazine. Haleiwa, Hawaii. Dec-Jan 1961
Photo: John Severson

Top: Don Hansen. Sunset Beach, Hawaii. 1961. Photo: Judy Rohloff
Center: Fresh lobster from Kawela Bay. With son Nicky and it looks like Australian surfing champion, Nat Young. Photo: Hansen collection
Bottom: More than 60 years ago, Don Hansen sat on this corner, hitchhiking toward his destiny. Photo: Ahrens

Top left: Don's mentor and lifelong friend, Robert Farr Driver.
Photo: Hansen collection
Top Right: Hansen's surf shop in Cardiff, where the Kraken now stands.
Photo: Hansen collection
Bottom Left: Don Hansen with boards he built start to finish.
Photo: Hansen collection
Bottom Right: Surf legend, L.J. Richards (L), Women's surfing pioneer Linda Benson, Don Hansen. Hansen Skateboard models made for L.J. and Linda. Photo: Hansen collection

Top right: Surfer Magazine ad. 1968. Photo: Hansen collection
Top left: Don with his number-one team rider, Mike Doyle. Photo: Keck
Bottom right: Hansen Surfer Magazine ad, circa 1965.
Photo: Hansen collection
Bottom left: Don surfing a small day at Cardiff Reef.
Photo: Hansen collection

148

Top left: Hansen family reunion. Photo: Hansen collection
Top right: Don & Shirley in work or at play. Photo: Hansen collection
Bottom left: Christian Hansen as a gremmie, with Menehune trophy. Photo: Hansen collection
Bottom right: Sage Hansen. Photo: Hansen collection

Top: Tiger Woods and his Hansen Surfboard. Photo: Hansen collection
Bottom: President Ronald Reagan about to go right with his Hansen Surfboard. Photo: Hansen collection

Don ready to jump, old-school style. Photo: Mike "godflicker" Anderson

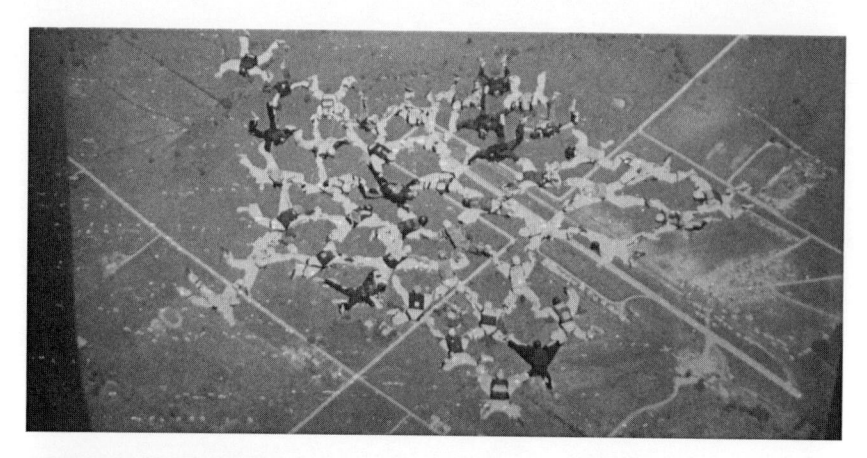

Top: World Speed Star record. 50 minus one.
Photo: Mike "godflicker" Anderson
Center: Don flying the flag for the company he helped found.
Photo: Mike "godflicker" Anderson
Bottom: Josh taking the drop. Photo: Hansen collection

Welcome to Montana. Photo: Hansen collection

Top: Hansen family Christmas in Big Sky. Photo: Hansen collection
Center: 1997 team roping competition. Photo: Ahrens
Bottom: Some things can't be tamed. Photo: Ahrens

Top: Don splitting logs near his home in Big Sky, Montana. Photo: Ahrens
Center: Don with Getaway (L) and Rivers. Photo: Ahrens
Bottom: Fred (L) and Barney. Photo: Ahrens

Top: Don in deep. Photo: Hansen collection
Center: Don and his daughter, Heidi on the trail. Photo: Hansen collection
Bottom: Don & Jerry Pape practicing team roping.
Photo: Hansen collection

Don Hansen's life is characterized by great joy. Photo: Hansen collection

CHAPTER SEVEN

The Long Drop

"You have to have a sense of humor about everything, even death."

My friend John Freeze wasn't really a skydiver. Still, he once strapped a parachute to himself and connected it to a bunch of helium balloons. They took him out to the desert, and he went up to 10,000 feet and began popping the balloons with a B.B. gun. He was trying to set some kind of a world record. He did it two or three times. He's a book in itself. As a kid, he was on the Hobie Skateboarding Team. Now he owns some nice restaurants in town.

But skydivers are kind of like surfers in a way; they're all half crazy. Surfers can take some significant risks, but for the most part, they are pretty calculated risks. Skydivers are a different breed.

By the early '70s I had four kids and was trying to keep our family together. Still, try as we did, Sharon and I ended up getting divorced. She was a nice woman, but we had really grown apart. I was still involved with the retail store and manufacturing, but I didn't have much time for surfing any longer. We made great surfboards and even made one for President Ronald Reagan that I'm sure was never ridden. The San Diego mayor at the time, Pete Wilson, got me to make that board. We also made a surfboard for Tiger Woods and Allen Bean, an astronaut who had been to the moon.

 My dad had been a pilot, and he helped restore the little airport in Redfield and got up and running again. Now small planes land there all the time, especially during hunting season. Through him, I became interested in flying planes and have all kinds of ratings—

THE LONG DROP

instrument ratings, multi engines, commercial licenses, everything. I have most of the ratings that commercial airline pilots have. In fact, I once flew a D-C 7 from San Diego to L.A. There were passengers on board, and the pilot let me fly it in all the way into where we needed the Instrument Landing System. He could have been fired for that, and I still can't believe he let me do it.

In a way jumping from a plane was like flying one. But I first tried skydiving because I got divorced and needed something to scare me just enough to get my mind off things. It was perfect, but I was worried about the leg I had damaged and wasn't sure if it would hold up after hitting the ground in a parachute. I had broken the same leg twice by then and would break it again years later when I tried ski racing. When I got it operated on, they took out a pin that had been in there since I was in high school, 40 years earlier. To test my leg, I went to the beach and jumped from about six feet into the sand. After a few tries, I knew it would hold, and I never did get hurt in any of my jumps.

HANSEN

When you jump out of that plane, you're not thinking of anything except making it safely to the ground. My divorce was the furthest thing from my mind when I was jumping. I did four jumps the first day, and I've done around 1,500 jumps overall. We were usually at 10,000 feet when we jumped from the plane, betting that our Army Surplus, World War II parachutes would open. They usually did, but there were times when they malfunctioned. This occurred about one out of every 500 jumps.

I had on an old Capewell rig [a Capewell is a hand-activated device for detaching the parachute harness from the canopy]. It was part of the old military equipment that was like 30-years-old at the time. Anyway, I went for my Capewell, and after one side came out, I was hanging sideways in the air. I remember thinking, *Okay, Hansen, slow down and do it right or you're gonna die.* Everything was a mess, wholly tangled and flopping around when I decided to get rid of it and get my reserve out. It was a real problem releasing

THE LONG DROP

those old parachutes when you're falling at 120 miles per hour, and your brain isn't working right. It wasn't like my entire life flashed before my eyes, but some events did come into clear focus. Time meant nothing in one sense, but I also realized that I had seconds to get my reserve parachute out. I finally got it right, and my reserve opened at around 500 feet, which is only a few seconds from bouncing.

I remember getting on the ground, and these guys were laughing their asses off, saying, "We thought you were gone." You develop a morbid sense of humor when you're dealing with the possibility of death all the time. Over time I've realized that you need a sense of humor about everything, even death.

I went on to captain *Airfreight*, a Ten-man speed star team. [Speed star completion is a timed event measured from when the first jumper exits the plane, and all ten jumpers link hands for two seconds or more. The first team to the ground wins]. Our team consisted of carpenters, laborers, machinists, mechanics, and people from different walks of life. We all had jobs, and so we did most of our jumps on the weekends. We eventually started entering competitions for the Ten Man Speed Star, something we would finally break several worlds records for. All aeronautic world records are kept in Paris, France, and we have some diplomas that record our world's records. It shows that at one time, we were the best Speed Star team in the world. I have a "Jump Master" rating that I never used. Being a Jump Master means you know where and when to send guys out of the plane.

No matter how often you jump, however, you never get entirely used to it. I was sitting in an airplane once with a guy from Salt Lake City who had around 10,000 jumps. I asked him, "Do you ever get scared?" He said, "I'm going through a period right now where I'm scared every time I get out the door." I was glad I wasn't the only one who felt that way.

One of the top skydivers and my close friend Dennis [Trepanier] once jumped when he was really hungover. He barfed on the way

THE LONG DROP

up. I found out first-hand that the quickest way to get over a hangover is to jump from 10,000 feet.

Dennis and I were out drinking one evening at this place on Coast Highway in Cardiff called the Hydra when we decided to jump onto the beach in front of the restaurant. By the time we jumped, it was long past dark. We pulled off the jump, but everything was shut down for the night by the time we landed on the beach. I can't remember why, but we didn't have a ride back to our cars, parked back at the airport. Maybe the guy who was supposed to take us back to the airport had left. Anyway, there we were, holding onto our skydiving equipment, when a sheriff approached us. I thought we were in trouble because we didn't have any permits for what we were doing—we never did have permits, really. Instead of questioning us about that, however, the sheriff asked us if we needed a ride. He drove us back to Palomar Airport.

Trepanier was a key member of our Speed Star team, and no matter what, you could count on him being right where he needed to be every time. Once we were about to get into this DC-3, and the pilot was hollering at us to hurry up. Dennis was walking in front of us when his reserve parachute fell onto the dusty ground. [The reserve is the chute you have in case your main chute fails to open.] I told him to lie down on his stomach while I put his reserve back in. I got to the last pin when one of the guys, I think it was Jeff Davey, said, "Don, I think you're putting the pin in the wrong way." We argued about it for a few minutes until Trepanier said, "Just put the fuckin' thing in and let's go." Well, Dennis had a malfunction on that jump, and I remember him going past me, fighting for his life, going for his reserve. When I saw his parachute blossoming below me at around 500 feet, which is seconds before you hit the ground, I breathed a great sigh of relief.

Dennis Trepanier picks up the story and tells his memories of some near fatalities while skydiving with Hansen.

THE LONG DROP

I first met Don at the drop zone. He was an organizer of the jumps during the weekend, and he invited me to one of his organized jumps. From then on, we became good friends and jumped almost every weekend together. He was older than most of us, but everyone in the group accepted him right away. He just had something about him that everyone was drawn to.

We weren't close enough to discuss personal issues at the time, so we never discussed his getting divorced. Four years later I was going to his next wedding and what a wedding it was!

I've had my life flash before my eyes on one of our team jumps. I had a malfunction on my main parachute, cut it away in my reserve failed to open. I reached back to pull my reserve open with both hands and got my reserve open at 300 feet. I actually saw the ground rushing up and saw my life flash before my eyes. Later on, I found out why my reserve didn't open—the loop that holds the pin for the parachute was hardened from the sun. All the nine jumpers on our team then laid their parachutes on the ground, pulled their reserves, and half stayed closed. Soon afterward, there was a recall of all those rigs we had been using.

A fellow jumper named Joe Garcia once organized a large formation to break the worlds record. While exiting the aircraft, my reserve opened and snagged on the airplane's tail, shredding it. I took my hook knife out, cut all 24 lines, and went back into free fall and pulled my main. Survived another one!

Whenever my chute doesn't open, I don't take time to think much; it's just a normal reaction for me to cut away and pull the reserve. I had malfunctions several times and found myself sitting under my reserve before realizing what I had done. It was purely on instinct.

We used ex-military parachutes that we modified to get forward speed out of them. They had a reserve mounted on the front ...real old school, and eventually, they would malfunction.

THE LONG DROP

> Hansen was very much a natural at jumping. Usually, it takes guys hundreds of jumps to get to where he got in a very short time. He was very athletic and was just one of those guys that had a knack for everything. When he decided to build a ten-Man Speed Star team, he invited me to join the team he captained. We won the National Parachuting Championships two years in a row, so he must have been good. I always felt safe jumping with Don. He was very conscientious and a safe jumper.

It's a good feeling knowing you can get through a malfunction, but once you see guys that don't make it and realize what can happen, it becomes more frightening. I never thought it would happen to Mike Anderson. He was a really good skydiver and knew precisely what he was doing. He took about half of the skydiving photos I have. We called him the "godflicker." On every jump where we attempted a world's record, he'd be on it, coming out after we jumped. He ended up dying by landing in Lake Elsinore and drowning. It shocked the hell out of me. The only thing we could figure out was that he was over his head somewhere, and he was trying to save all his big, heavy camera equipment. Lake Elsinore's a really shallow lake, and I figure he was so stubborn that he tried to keep his camera equipment.

Jeff Davey is a great skydiver and the tenth man out on Airfreight's Ten Man Speed Star. The 10th man out has to be the quickest on the team. He has to get out quickly, fly fast, and know-how to hook up with the star without taking everyone out. According to Davey:

I met Don sometime in early '75 when we made some jumps at the Elsinore Drop Zone. My logbook shows we made our first *team* jump on March 30, 1975.

You've got to understand that skydivers are unique. The only things we all have in common is that we were all seeking the ultimate adrenaline rush. It didn't matter your race, sex, nationality, or sexual orientation. Everybody knew about it, but that or your financial situation, none of it mattered to anyone. Still, if you were loaded, you could afford to make many jumps and have state of the art gear. You had a range of guys from low life druggies to company CEOs jumping right next to each other. The mode of transportation to or from the drop zone ranged from hitchhiking to driving whatever car we had to the drop zone and back.

We all came from different backgrounds, but everyone is the same once you are in freefall. Everyone falls at 180 plus feet per second. Don was a naturally charismatic leader and organizer. Many on the team referred to him as "Daddy Don." He was well-liked by most, especially guys like me, who always bummed smokes off him. He'd bitch about it, saying, "Davey you cheap son of a bitch," but he never turned me down. Sandy Doyle coined our team's name, "Airfreight." We became two-time National Champions, and we continue to hold the FAI World Record for the Ten-Man Speed Star.

You could fill an entire book on the times when you are in trouble skydiving and your life flashes before your eyes. You think, *Oh shit, I'm going to die!* Actually, that's just part of the experience. Your adrenaline is already at peak pressure when you are ready to pull, and you've got around ten seconds to successfully deal with a problem or die; it's that simple. Your training takes over, and depending on how well you practiced your emergency procedures, you live or die. Most make it, a few don't.

Early on, all of us learned using military surplus equipment. It didn't work every time, and they really sucked at times and were a pain to work with. Don knew that, but he kept at it. Mike Parnell created the phrase "Don Hansen, the weathervane man, he spins, turns, gets in." Don exited in the seventh position, which could be challenging at times. It's easy to get twisted around. But Don was in the top one percent of skydivers in the world. He could recruit and hold onto the top point-one percent in the world. On the ski slopes, he

THE LONG DROP

> kicked my ass, no way I could keep up with him. Like all world-class athletes, he thrived under pressure.

In skydiving, you have your main chute and a reserve. If something goes wrong, and you can't get your chute out, you need to use your reserve. The reserve used to be mounted on the belly in the old days, and when I had to use it once, it nearly broke me in two. I couldn't find my ripcord, and I had to go for my reserve. I watched that thing snake up real slow. I was relieved, but the thing just about busted me in half. The brakes slam on in a hurry. I couldn't walk for a week; my back was so screwed up.

I've seen five or six guys get killed after a malfunction. I watched them go right into the ground from a distance. As I said, skydiving is kind of a morbid sport—you see someone fighting for his life, trying to get his reserve out, and all you can do is laugh. It's a nervous laugh, trying to distract yourself. We always figured the guy was gonna make it, but the few times they didn't, the laughing stopped.

But I would never go over to look at the body of someone who didn't make it. I once had two good friends killed in one jump. I was standing by the brother of one of the guys. He and another jumper were tangled and fell, and he asked me, "Was that Rick?" I told him no, I didn't think so, but I knew it was.

After this tragic accident, they shut down that drop zone for the next few hours. We were practicing for The Nationals, so we went to a different airfield, from Paris, California, to Lake Elsinore. We were making another jump within two or three hours. I was sitting in that airplane thinking how weird it was that we were jumping right after a friend of ours was killed.

The real danger in skydiving is not so much jumping, but the planes you're flying in—at least the ones we flew in were old pieces of shit. We took off one time in an old Canadian rotary engine airplane. One of Canada's contributions to aviation was a floatplane called the Beaver, but we would also jump from DC3's and Beech D-18's. I don't recall the

THE LONG DROP

type of plane we were in at the time, but it had come out before the Beaver, and the Beaver was first built in 1947. I remember taking off, and all of a sudden, the windshield was covered in oil. Not a great time to discover that there's an oil leak in the engine. The guy had to throttle back and take us around again while we're hoping he could see well enough to land. I had two or three friends killed in plane wrecks.

I once had a girlfriend, Sally Miller, who was a jumper. She went on this jump over Los Angeles with eight other women. The first person out of the plane is called the "floater." The floater gets out the door and hangs on in the wind stream, opening up their bodies and floating down to the star. The moment the star starts forming, the group floats slower and slower. A woman named Mary was the floater this one day. She got out of the plane, which was an old Beech D-18. Now, I'm not sure if it was her reserve or main, but one of her chutes came out of the bag, blew up, and wrapped around one of the Beech D-18's dual rudders. The plane was porpoising through the sky, and the other women were still in the plane screaming when they saw her chute open inadvertently and hang up on the tail. They were shouting, "Oh my God, what are we gonna do; we gotta help Mary!" Mike Anderson, the skydiving photographer I mentioned earlier, was in the back of the plane. He looked around at everyone and said, "You can't help Mary; Mary's on her own." Get out of this plane, or you're all gonna die. If you don't jump, I'm coming out the door over you whether you jump or not."

Mary hadn't gotten knocked out, but she had broken her arm and done a lot of damage to herself. She had a knife on her that she used to cut away her chute and get it loose from the plane. Her chute fell away, and she opened her reserve. She was fine, and a couple weeks later, she was out jumping again with a cast on her arm.

The most significant damage came to the airplane and the pilot. He was so shaken up that when he got back to Paris Airport, he ground

THE LONG DROP

looped it on landing and tore the shit out of the airplane. [In *aviation*, a *ground loop* is a rapid rotation of a fixed-wing *aircraft* while on the *ground*.]

Roger Kersey was part of the Airfreight's Ten-Man Speed Star team. According to Hansen, he is a great skydiver and a really nice guy. According to Kersey:

Controlling your body in freefall is a learned skill. Once information with other jumpers, the formation takes on a unique aerodynamic presence. It must be flown, like one individual body. The mantra for us became "smoother, cleaner, faster." Early jumps were made from 13,000 feet, giving the group a full minute to make the star. Timing the jump in competition begins when the first jumper is visible out the door of the airplane. The time is set when the 10th jumper enters the formation. From there, the star must be held an additional two seconds to count as a valid time.

Our times began to come down as we gained experience. From 45 seconds in 1967 to 25 seconds by the early '70s. Teams took on different names, and our team was named "Airfreight." The team was assembled in 1976, and practice started in the winter, looking to compete in the National Championships in Oklahoma that coming June. That first year, we finished 5th out of more than 20 teams, not too shabby for a team without much experience, compared to most of the others. By the spring of 1977, we were making 10-man stars cleanly in 13 to 15 seconds. Once we got to "smoother, cleaner, faster," everything seemed to come naturally.

By then, most of our jumps were made from 7,500 feet, a 30-second freefall. Why waste all that airplane time and money for a 60-second freefall? When our times started getting consistently into the 11's, Don's idea was to drop the exit altitude to 5,500 feet for a 20-second freefall! He asked me for my opinion, and I said I was all in.

THE LONG DROP

There's more pressure, and the ground looks much closer from 5,500 feet compared to 7,500. Some team members weren't too happy with that, but everyone finally agreed to try it. The first few jumps were disastrous due to the added tension of knowing we had less time. We stuck with 5,500 feet, and soon the stars began forming cleanly again. And the times started falling: 11.2, 10.6, 10.2!

We knew we had a shot at the Russian record by then, which they held for years. In Oklahoma, in June, we competed in the Nationals. We blew the first jump, but the judge's view was obscured because we were behind a cloud, so we were awarded a re-jump, and this time we didn't screw up. Our times were consistently in the 9-10 second range. We won the National 10-Man Star Championship. After the event was completed, USPA (National body and Nationals organizers) sponsored two jumps with international judges watching so we could go for the Russian record. The team voted unanimously to try from 5500 feet. I think we had a 9.8 on the first and a 9.4 on the second jump. A new world record was ours!

World Records

We broke every record in our category at the time. We then submitted everything to the *Federation Aeronatique* in Paris, France, where they were verified. That award was really gratifying, as was winning the Nationals two years in a row. But those drop zones are in dismal places for the most part. All you can do there is jump. After one event, someone said, "Airfreight was the fastest in the sky and the fastest to get out of town afterward." We didn't even stick around to pick up the medals. They had to send them to us.

We did many demo jumps, and I clearly remember jumping onto the football field at San Dieguito High School in Encinitas once. I don't know how we did that with all those wires overhead. I drive by there now, look and think, *What were we thinking?*

One day some of the guys on my team and I were doing a demo jump over an elementary school in Encinitas. Military smoke bombs

THE LONG DROP

are what we used. We'd buy a case of surplus smoke bombs, jump from the plane, pull the pin on the canister, and it would release the smoke so you could follow the first jumper down. You get out of the airplane and pull the pin from the canister. When you see the smoke, you follow the jumper down.

We couldn't find anything that was just smoke for our jump, so this guy sold us a case of smoke bombs with smoke on one side and W.P. (white phosphorous) on the other side. If you get that shit on you, it will burn right through you, all the way to your bones. It was dangerous to have, but we were young and dumb, so we went for it and made this jump. There were four of us on the jump, and only one guy wore the canister of smoke and W.P. We got done, and we were packing our parachutes on the ground at the school. I picked up the canister from the guy but forgot that the W.P. side of it was still alive. The only thing that had gone off was the smoke end of the canister. I had the canister in my parachute, and some kid walked up to me and asked if he could have the expended canister that the smoke had been in. I said, "Sure, you can have it," and I gave it to him. I went on packing my parachute, and about five minutes later, I thought, *What the hell did I do? The phosphorous part of the canister is still live!* All he had to do was pull the pin out of the other end of the canister I gave him, and it would be burning through everything. Boy, I tell you, it scared the living shit out of me. School was just letting out when I jumped up. About six buses lined up out in front of the school, waiting to take kids home. I went to the very first bus driver and said, " Don't move until … "I didn't even tell anyone what was going on. I went back through the buses, and on the third bus back, I asked again, "Who's the kid I gave that smoke canister to?" The kid raised his hand and said, "Yeah, I'm here." I got it back from him, and fortunately, he hadn't done anything. That could have been a real disaster.

Another time that I had the hell scared out of me was when I was making a jump at a

THE LONG DROP

school in Cardiff. I couldn't find anyone who had ever flown a "jumper" before, so someone said, "I know a woman with a commercial license; she'll take you." She had a Cherokee-180 or something. I thought *I'll wear smoke for this one jump.* I didn't usually like wearing smoke cause it was one more thing for the parachute to hang upon. I got out of the airplane and pulled the pin before I slid out. I was jumping alone. The smoke didn't go off right away, which happens sometimes, but usually, it goes off five or ten seconds later. Without thinking, I took the canister off my leg because I didn't like wearing it and threw it back into the airplane. Right then, I went, *What did I just do? If that thing hesitates and goes off in the plane, the cockpit's gonna fill with smoke, and that woman won't have a clue what's happening.* I was twisting around in the sky, trying to stay stable and see the airplane again. Fortunately, it didn't go off; it was a dud. Those were the two worst mistakes I ever made, and they had to do with smoke.

It was frightening; I could have killed both those people.

I am honored to have captained a team that was the best in the world. We practiced whenever we could, mostly on weekends, and were made of a group consisting of everyone from lawyers to laborers. With that, we won two National Championships and set every world record there was for the Ten-Man Speed Star. We once did a 49-man jump, it was supposed to have been 50, but one of the members didn't make it. After that, it was time to move on. Our ten-man team included: Ron Delmazzo, Mike Blood, Steve Parker, Mike Parnell, Dennis Trepanier, Jay Blood, Roger Kersey, Jim Edwards, Jeff Davey, Rich Pfeiffer and me.

CHAPTER EIGHT

Another Big Sky

A woman I met in Big Sky, Montana asked me where my love for horses began. She thought it started back in South Dakota when I worked on farms. But I didn't get involved with horses until I moved to Montana when I was 54-years-old.

Scott Foster is a team roper and ski friend with Don. He runs the local ski shop in Big Sky called "Lone Mountain Sports." According to Don, "Scott's a real cowboy. He team ropes and works cattle at times." According to Foster:

The best way to sum up my relationship with Don Hansen is to consider him as Tom Sawyer.

He is always getting people around him to do things they might not ordinarily do. We all thought it was fun to do these things because Don made it sound fun or beneficial for us, even though it was usually more advantageous for him. [Laughs] I first met him in Big Sky, Montana, in the late '80s. Don was just starting to ride horses and wanted to take pack trips up into the mountains. I took him on his first few trips.

Because of Don's new interest in horses, he also got into team roping. One time Don bought a new horse from South Dakota. He was a little nervous about the horse and conned me into riding him first. The horse bucked me off and stepped on my back. Eventually, we all had got a good laugh out of that. Tom Sawyer.

Don's addiction to adventure made him consider ski racing. As it turned out, he wasn't very good at it. He fell so hard that he broke his leg, [for the third time] along with five ribs, his shoulder, and collarbone. I went down to check on him as the ski patrol was taking him off the mountain. He was in such pain that I turned white and had to leave. After that, he said later that I was off his "In case of emergency" friend list. The main thing I get from Don Hansen is his immense love of life and adventure. He is always up to something.

Team Roping

Jerry Pape is a close friend of mine most of the time, but we've been through some times together. Pape's father, Frank, was a really famous cop in Chicago. I didn't believe him at first when he told me that, but he showed me a wedding picture of him and his wife, and there's Mayor Daley in the background. There's a book about Frank Pape titled "The Toughest Cop in America." Maybe that's where Jerry gets it.

There are three chutes in team roping: The left one is for the header, the middle one for the steer, and the right one is for the heeler. I was the header, and Pape was the healer. When they give you the go sign, the steer shoots out of the box, the header tries to come out at the same time and tries to rope him as quickly as possible. The idea is to get him roped on the head, dally around your saddle horn, and turn him around the corner. That's when the heeler comes in and heels him and stretches him, and that's the end of the event. It's timed, and everything happens really quickly.

Jerry and I won the Big Sky team roping competition held at the 320 Ranch Rodeo in 1997. It's a small-town rodeo and not a really big deal, but there were still some good ropers there. However, the most prominent team-roping event I ever won was with John Cooney. It was a draw pot where I was the header and drew an excellent healer. That was the Park County Roping Championship in Livingston, Montana, which is right in the middle of cowboy country. That was a big deal—I won a saddle and a thousand bucks.

It's expected that injuries will occur in team roping, but unexpected things can happen even on the trail. I was once riding

ANOTHER BIG SKY

with this woman on a really tough trail, up to a lake. I had a great trail horse, but he somehow tripped and fell, and I landed on a pile of rocks. I landed hard and was knocked out for five or ten seconds. That can happen any time you come off a horse that hard. Once I came to and got my wits about me, I saw the woman standing over me saying, "Are you all right, Don; are you all right?" I noticed that the horse was still lying on his back, struggling in a pile of deadfall. I walked toward him, and before I knew it, he was back on the trail, just standing there. My friend asked me if she should go for help because it was obvious I was in bad shape. I could stand up, but barely. We were in a place with many bears, and I didn't have bear spray, a gun, or anything. I thought *I'll be bear bait if I'm lying here by myself for two or three hours.* I forced myself to walk down the trail about 50 yards until I couldn't go any further. I somehow had to get on that horse and ride out. I still don't know how I did it, but I finally rode the two or three miles to the trailhead.

My friend was behind me the entire time, saying, "Don, are you all right; are you all right?" It must have looked like I was falling asleep as I rode. I couldn't move when we got to the trailhead, not even to get off the horse. Finally, some hikers helped lift me off the horse. When I got back into cell range, I called Jerry's Pape's wife, and she came down and picked me up. The biggest mistake I made was saying, "Take me to the Big Sky Emergency Room." If we had gone directly to Bozeman, it would have saved me a $1,500 ambulance ride. As soon as we got to a hospital, they put me in an ambulance and sent me to Bozeman anyway.

Everyone needs someone to teach them the ropes when they go to a new environment. My son's godfather, Pete Adams, who died a few years ago, taught Joshua, and I'm sure he taught him about all the bad things we did when we were younger. The guy who taught me all the old-time trails around Big Sky is a cowboy named Chuck Ankeny. Chuck's dad had been the cow boss at the

ANOTHER BIG SKY

Flying D Ranch, which Ted Turner bought in the 1960s, I believe. Chuck got us on a wrong heading once in the mountains. About four of us were on that ride, and the only way out of there was on a ridge. We were in an area with some steep cliffs around, and I wasn't sure we could get back up if we got stuck in there. Finally, we got to a spot that had been logged years earlier. Then I knew there had to be a way out of there if people had been there before. It was a relief to find our way out of that canyon because I was afraid we would get stuck down there. Eventually, if you can't get out, you have to walk, leave your horses, and hope they find their way out on their own.

    Even after I learned to ride, it took me five years before some of these old cowboys would acknowledge me. There are still some real cowboys left in Montana, and they bust their asses in their work.

    I spent 10 or 12 years team roping, and I even roped a lot in Hawaii. Captain Cook first brought the cattle to Hawaii in the 1700s. The Mexican vaqueros took care of them. When

I tell guys in Montana that there were cattle in Hawaii before they were in Montana, they don't believe me. I roped with many Mexican guys whose families had been in Hawaii for over 200 years.

I'm cautious now, even with skiing. I can't afford any more broken bones, believe me. I can't even count how many I've had but at least three broken legs, a broken hand, collarbones, and a countless number of ribs. Every time I go off a horse, I'll break some ribs or collapse a lung. I found out that you could still breathe with one lung; you don't even realize you have a collapsed lung. Collapsing both of them is not such a good idea. Even so, I wouldn't do anything differently.

I have no clue how many bones I've broken, but, among others, at least nine or ten ribs. Every time I've been bucked off a horse or had it stumble and fall, I've broken ribs. The first thing that hits the ground is your ass; the next thing is your head. In between, it gets at least two or three ribs. I've had three collapsed lungs. One of the times I refused to go to the hospital because I had been in there so many times, and I knew I could live with a collapsed lung. They wanted to take me to the hospital, and I asked the doctor, "If I go home and sleep in my own bed, am I gonna die?" She said, "Probably not." So I went home and went to sleep. About one in the morning, I had to take a leak. When I couldn't get out of bed, Shirley had to get up and help me out, and then she called the ambulance.

Jerry Pape is Don's team roping partner, close friend, and main antagonist. Jerry had this to say about their numerous adventures and misadventures together:

When Hansen first got to town, he hung out with all the rich assholes. We were about a hundred years old when we started competing in team roping and about 200 when we quit.

I had been bucked off my horse once, chasing elk. I broke a few ribs, and the next day, I tied up my ribs with a thick belt and went with Hansen to a rodeo we were competing in. We didn't win any money. Afterward, when I was loading my horse into the trailer, I threw some alfalfa hay into the manger. When I did, my horse sneezed and blew hay into my face. That made me sneeze, and it put me on the trailer floor. When Don showed up, he asked me what the hell I was doing on the floor, between the horses.

I told him to grab the baseball bat from my truck and knock me out if I started sneezing again. He thought I was kidding. The next time Don went down with broken ribs and a collapsed lung, I told him I was getting a pen and paper to write down which of his things I wanted before he died.

Don is unique because he has no ego, even though he should have with all he's done. He can't have a big ego around me. I help keep him humble by always telling him what an incompetent asshole he is [Laughs].

After hearing Pape's description of their "friendship," Don had this to say: "Pape is the biggest egomaniac I've ever known. I can't believe some of the things he tells people. He wears his hat, boots, and his big belt buckle whenever he goes anywhere. These older tourist women came up to him once and asked, "Excuse me, are you a rancher? " He's no rancher, but he said, 'Yeah.' When they asked if he had any cattle, he said, 'Yeah , I own cattle.' At that point, I got up and left because I knew he was referring to the eight roping steers we had leased for the summer. I'm sure he gave those women a big story after I left.

I love going to the rodeo and was supposed to go to the National Finals Rodeo (NFR) this year in Las Vegas. [The NFR was canceled in 2020 due to Covid.] The NFR has grown to become one of the most significant events in Las Vegas. But even if they did hold the rodeo, I couldn't attend this year because of a leg injury. The riders there are so good it's unbelievable. Team roping is a timed event, and these guys are just unbelievably fast.

HANSEN

I always wanted to go on a trail drive but never had the opportunity. I was supposed to go once, but something came up. So, I loaned my horses to a guy who was going on a drive to celebrate Montana's 200th anniversary. A historic trail drive is challenging to reenact anymore because now there are fences everywhere.

Ski Racing

My friend Harry Ring taught me ski racing. I was in my mid-50s, but I wanted to try it. Harry was a far better ski racer than I could have ever been. He was on the Montana State Nordic Racing Team.

According to Ring:

Big Sky was a small town when we first met the Hansens. Don was great at a party, and he fit right into the group. It quickly became apparent that he was a risk-taker but a calculated risk-taker who sometimes got more than he bargained for. You've got to know that any time you hook up with Don, it's likely to be an adventure. We were once completely lost riding horses in Yellowstone after dark. But he had done thousands of parachute jumps, so I doubt he thought twice about anything like ski racing or roping a steer from a horse, even in middle age. Actually, middle age was young compared to some locals such as Fred Pearl, Chuck Ankeny, and others. We were lucky to have them as role models.

I really enjoyed skiing, and I became a decent skier, not great. I love the adrenaline of going fast and always wanted to race. I ran this racecourse a few times in Big Sky called Big Horn. The guy who was starting me, Bob Dible, was an experienced downhiller. As I was preparing to go, he turned to me and said, "Now Hansen, don't let it all out on this first run; take it a little slower at first." Big Horn is not a difficult course—it has a shallow start and then the first drop off where you pick up speed. I told myself that I would stay in my tuck through the entire top steep section, but I probably shouldn't have done that.

HANSEN

I hit this roller at the bottom of the run called "the Big Horn Bump," or something like that. I was probably doing 60 or 70 miles an hour at the time, but I didn't put a big enough move on my turn. You've got to know what you're doing, which I did not. All of a sudden, I was about 15 feet in the air, thinking, *Oh shit, I'm screwed!* I remember being in mid-air, thinking I should hold my tuck all the way to the ground. I did that, but in hindsight, I would have been better off if I had opened up. You bleed off about 20 miles an hour if you open up like that. I was thinking I could land it, and I held my tuck. The next thing I knew, I was sitting on the side of the course with a shattered shoulder blade, a broken collarbone, three or four broken ribs, a broken leg I had broken twice before, and a punctured lung. My lying there on the ground held up the race for a full hour.

Scott Foster seems to remember it differently, but from my memory, he took one look at me and skied off. After that, a man named Peter, a complete stranger, stopped and sat there with me. I was feeling all right until I started to spasm. Peter stayed there with me, holding my hand. When you're hurting like that, it's comforting to know that someone's looking out for you.

I knew Olympic ski racer Andy Mill pretty well. He was a top downhiller. I saw him at the ski show after my racing accident, and he said, "Hansen, what the hell were you thinking, racing at your age? "I've run all the courses in the world, and I don't think I could run a downhill now." He was probably 45 at the time, and I was around 55. I always thought I was in control of whatever I did and was never really worried about getting hurt when I was having fun. Judging by all my injuries, I guess I wasn't always in control. [Laughs]

One thing I would have done differently in life is not run downhills in my mid-50s. I continued skiing after that accident, but I didn't race anymore. That one really laid me up and ended my so-called racing career. Instead of racing, I went helicopter skiing. I never had a close call, but I did get buried up to my waist a couple times. That isn't really that big a deal, but it's tough getting free when it happens. The minute the slide stops, the snow starts to solidify. I never got caught in one big enough to scare me, though.

    The only other time I got hurt skiing was when I took a lesson running gates from an instructor. I was one of the last guys to run the course and was standing sideways on the hill. We were waiting for the very last guy to come through. He still had one gate left, but he didn't make it, and when he slipped, he came sliding right toward me, going fast. He took my skis right out from under me, and I went down and broke my collarbone. I just heard the whole thing crack. I thought, *Oh shit; here we go again.*

I like to get as far as I think I can with my abilities, and then I can taper off or even quit the sport if it starts looking too dangerous. Even in skydiving, I got about as good as I figured I could. It got kind of boring going up

ANOTHER BIG SKY

in a plane, falling through the sky, and hoping your parachute would open. After a while, the best thing about skydiving was having a few beers afterward.

One of my only other regrets in sports is not playing college football. I was an all-state football player during my junior year in high school, and I figured I could have gone on to play for a small college. But you need a body utterly different than mine for football. I have these skinny little legs that are always breaking.

CHAPTER NINE

Family Business

I've enjoyed going to work for my entire life. I've been working at the shop for over 60 years, and I've never become tired of it. I tell all of our young employees that regardless of what you do, it has to be something where you can get up each day for the rest of your life and enjoy it. If that's not gonna happen, don't do it. It can be a struggle, but I keep telling them to just put one foot ahead of the other one. If you're smart enough, do a good enough job and work hard enough, you're probably gonna be successful. I don't care what anybody says; there's a lot of luck involved. Other than that, it all comes down to hard work.

When I started my business, I would shape all day for Hobie in Dana Point before driving home to Cardiff to shape until early morning. I worked like that for an entire summer and made about 10 to 12 boards a month and sold them for about $110.00. The sacrifice came, and they're always a sacrifice, that I didn't surf much that summer. I was always too tired. You have to follow your dreams; don't get locked into something you don't like. If you do, you're gonna be stuck there for the rest of your life.

 I worked without a safety net at times. You might be better off not having the safety net of partnership because partnerships don't always work. In fact, they very seldom run smoothly. You see people go into partnership, and over the years, they end up hating each other. They split up, and the business goes to hell. I was lucky that the guy who became my partner ... he chose me, I guess. He mentored me and loaned me money; he was a great guy. I give kids as much advice as I can. I don't mind guys going into the surfboard business around here; I figure the least I can do is help them out when I can. I've been good at getting

FAMILY BUSINESS

people started by giving them their first job. We've had hundreds of people who got their first job here at Hansen's. I have lots of them coming back to me all the time. It makes me feel good like I've accomplished something; it's not like I'm changing the world, but I've given many young kids a good start in their working life. And some of the awards I've received have meant a lot, like The Silver Surfer Award I received from the California Surf Museum. I was up on the stage with Tommy Curren and Lisa Anderson. That made me feel really cool.

I think having a mentor is really important. I've had people tell me I was their mentor at times, but I wasn't the type of mentor that I had. Trust me when I say I've been far from perfect. [At this point, Hansen lifts his sleeve to prove his point and reveal a tattoo of a rectangular box and the initials "DH" within it.] This was done probably in 1951 or '52, the South Dakota State Fair. The guy took it from a dirty case, wiped it off with some toilet paper, and stuck it in my arm. I've actually thought of having someone put some sort of design over it, so it looks like something. My mother cried when she saw it. My dad looked at it and said, "Oh, Don." [Laughs]

The following is taken from a conversation between Don's wife, Shirley, and their youngest son, Josh:

Shirley: Don is really good at holding things together when everything seems to be falling apart. However, I think one of his best qualities is relinquishing responsibility to people and then treating them like family. We've been so blessed. We have seven people who have been here for 45 years and many others who have been here for 35 years. The true crew hasn't changed much, and that's what gave us the ability to move to Montana. I didn't want to go; I was totally against it. I had grown up in Ohio and had all the snow I wanted. But that became one of our best memories.
Josh: It's funny you say it that way, cause I

heard you wanted to go to Montana and Dad wanted to stay.

Shirley: No, that was years earlier. By the time we left, Don wanted a place in the mountains. We went for the summer, and the business didn't fall apart. We found that the employees could handle it, and that gave us the confidence to move away. It's funny how there are different memories of that time.

His relationship with Bob Driver showed me everything I needed to know about him. They were partners and best friends. Bob was the best man at our wedding. Everyone called him Bob, but Don respected him so much that he called him Mister Driver until the day he died. I remember Don struggling with dissolving their partnership.

Josh: They had been partners on the manufacturing side of Hansen's. When they transferred into retail, their business wasn't doing that well at first. They were 50/50 partners, and one year Don bought all this ski gear for the shop. Driver came in and said, "Don, you've broken us; this will never work." Don told Mister Driver he thought it was time to split up their partnership." Bob said, "Sure, we should." Six months later, all that ski stuff was sold, and the business was thriving.

Shirley: Don ran bus trips to the snow before that. He tells the stories about the bus sliding off the road and all that when they drove to Mammoth. It was never about the money for Don or Bob, but Bob didn't want to finalize the breakup. Don was so much like Bob, and even when the business was small, we were loaning money to people to buy their first homes. We traveled with the Drivers; they were really like family.

Josh: Dad always preached staying calm regardless of what's happening. We would go through times when we'd be down thousands of dollars a day and think we were going to be hurt badly. No matter what, however, he was always about putting his head down. He's calm but conservative in business. On December 10th every year, he would say pretty much the same thing.

FAMILY BUSINESS

Shirley: We're gonna go broke; there's no snow.

Josh: That sort of mentality has helped him when things got tough. But even when his surfboard business was going under, he would keep moving forward, get work done and not feel sorry for himself. In skydiving and any of his other experiences, you can't freak out. I've had to cutaway [disconnect the main parachute in preparation for opening the reserve parachute], so I know what he means.

Shirley: In his mind, he wasn't doing anything dangerous in skydiving. To him, skydiving or golfing are all the same.

Josh: When you eventually do those things, there's a risk. You always have to be prepared, and he was ready. He would think way ahead, sometimes maybe to a fault. But he's always been interested in lifestyle over money.

Shirley: Yes, it was always about lifestyle; money was never his driver. When I married him, I didn't know him as a surfer until we started traveling. Then it didn't matter if we were in Mexico or on a beach in the Caribbean, somebody would come up and say, "Don Hansen, I know you." He was skydiving when you were a few months old. There were several different accidents out there, not with him, but with people we knew. I finally said I didn't want the memory of him not making it, and I don't want the children to have that memory either.

Josh: They call it burning in.

Shirley: I told him we weren't going to any more of his jumps, and about a month later, he quit. But no matter what it is, when he goes, he goes 100 percent.

Josh: He is unique in that he can assimilate into any group, but he tends to gravitate toward the more colorful, unique people.

Shirley: Jerry Pape comes to mind. Ninety percent of the time, those two act like they're 12 years old. [Laughs] After Don plowed Pape's driveway in so nobody could get out, Jerry put a sign in our front yard with our phone number on it that said, "Bad construction; selling cheap!" [Laughter] It keeps life interesting.

FAMILY BUSINESS

Josh: Don once took $300 from Jerry's desk. The money had come from a guy who owed it to Jerry and put it on his desk. After Dad took the cash, he bought Jerry a gift with his own money. [Hard Laughter] Jerry said, "This is so nice of you, Don." There was a whole side shit show going on when the guy told Jerry he had put the money on his desk, and Jerry didn't believe him.

Shirley: Everyone's relationships were going down the tube while those two are having fun. But they've done some fantastic things together, including team roping and ski racing. Joshua, you got us through the Covid disaster by doing all the right things.

Josh: That was because I learned from a father who was very conservative and solid in business. He always told me to keep lots of money in my accounts in case someone needed it someday. That day came, and we did need it. It's easy to be in charge when things are great, but when the shit hits the fan …

It's an interesting dichotomy with Dad—he's such a hard charger and so cautious in business. He's always taught me that life can be very unpleasant and downright challenging at times. He won't like hearing this, but I think he has a big ego. Inevitably you can't be the person he is without one. He manages it really well. He's the nicest guy in the world and does things for other people that we sometimes can't believe.

Shirley: He doesn't have an ego with me. He doesn't want to tell everyone what he's done. It's like [Bob] Driver would have said, "If people think I've done something good, let *them* tell you about it, not me." For him, it's fun, but he's honored when someone thinks highly of him. Before I met Don, I hung out with many professional athletes who walked around, expecting you to know them. He's never had an ego like that.

Josh: As he's gotten older, he enjoys that people appreciate his legacy.

Shirley: Twenty years ago, he could have cared less, but I think he's become more interested in his legacy.

Josh: He has the good type of ego where he's

confident. So many people come back and tell me how Dad helped them out. He would always ask me to do the right thing, to be honest.

Shirley: I always think of that time in the park. The water was turned off in the hotel, and Don pulled in and told the guy at the kiosk that we were just going to ride around. He backed up and said, "We want to use the facilities; I'm sorry I lied to you."

Josh: He once tried to get the Kamaaina rate in Hawaii at a gold tournament by pretending to be Bill White. One of the guys driving a cart knew who Dad was but pretended not to know him. The guy finally said, "Don, I know who you are."

Shirley: One thing he doesn't do well is lie.

Josh: No, we've built our reputation on honesty and surfboards. But over time, we didn't have very many surfboards in the shop, and that's not what the community wanted from us. I told Don, "It says 'Hansen Surfboards' on our sign." But one of the reasons we've been so successful is that Don tried many different things, including camping

> gear and tennis. Now we've kind of gone full circle with our boardroom. The community has embraced that. There was an intangible value in surfboards that even Don had kind of lost track of.

Business Challenges

One thing that continues to motivate me is to influence the kids who work for us. I make a point of trying to get to know them. Sometimes they ask me for advice. And over the years, many of our employees have become like family to us. I'm not sure what we would do without them. I consider all of them irreplaceable.

Still, business can be competitive no matter what, and it can be stressful whenever the business changes, as it often does. Our son Josh knows that with Covid, and he passed that test with flying colors. My first big challenge is when boards went short, and the '60s and people began making their own boards. Still, I was young, and I knew I could do anything I wanted. I had to sell some property I didn't want to sell to survive, but we got through it.

FAMILY BUSINESS

When I first ordered skis, Driver walked into the store and saw everything I had ordered for ski season. It was probably $100,000 worth of products. He looked around and said, "I think you've broken us, Don." I thought about it a minute, but I didn't have any choice. We still had a couple pieces of property together, and I said, "Why don't I buy you out, cause I think this is the way we have to go." Turns out I was right, and all I can say is that I was fortunate. We farmed out surfboard production and got entirely out of manufacturing at that time, and went all-in on retail.

I had tried to buy ski equipment in September to sell in November, December, and January. Everyone else does their buying in January, seven months before you sell it. Everyone said, "Don, you're taking a big risk here; it's probably not going to work. But I managed to sell enough of it to pay for it all. When it did, I bought Driver out. I jockeyed some properties around and giving him some of them. I was so lucky.

HANSEN

There was no backup plan if it didn't work. I just kept putting one foot in front of the other and telling myself that it had to work. It was really a do or die situation. I'm not sure what I would have done if it didn't work.

We had no idea how big skiing would get for us. But we are only two hours from the slopes in Big Bear, and a lot of beach people wanted to ski and snowboard. That was one of the first significant disagreements I ever had with my business partner, Bob Diver.

Pami Bennett began working at Hansen's in 1993.
The following are some of her memories from those times:

When we first put gravel rocks in the back parking lot, nobody wanted to park there because it got our cars dirty. I didn't park there, and Don was pissed about it. I was downstairs in the lady's section when he spotted me and yelled my name, "Pami!" He bolted down the stairs as fast as a 70-year-old could. He's broken his legs a couple of times, and one of them looks like a wooden pirate leg. I ducked down under a clothing rack, figuring he couldn't find me. So now he's down looking for me, searching the racks, and I'm giggling because he can't catch me. Soon Don and I are laughing, and he can hear me as I crawl on the floor on my hands and knees. By the time he caught up with me, we were both laughing so hard we couldn't stop.

    Years ago, a cowboy with two horses was riding through town on his way to Mexico. He stopped at Hansen's, and Don said he could stay in our back lot, on the gravel. Don went and got him some hay for the horses. The guy was cool, John Wayne. He left early one morning, and Don really wanted to say goodbye to him. I can't remember what they said, but we had someone take our picture in front of the Cardiff Kook: Cowboy, Don, Kook, and me.

Marie "La" Tessieri is basically known as the person in charge of everything. She had this to say about her 42 years at Hansen's:

I believe it was the spring of 1977 when I first met Don. My good friends lived down here in Encinitas, and I used to come down from Hermosa Beach to visit them. They would have these great potluck Easter parties and an Easter egg hunt for the kids. I am sure I met him at one of these parties at Jerry Sherk's house in Cardiff. Don's wife, Shirley, and he had just started dating. It was a small world because I had known her a few years prior through people back east in Buffalo and Cleveland. They brought Don's kids to the Easter party, and that is where I met all of them—Christian, Heidi, and Sage.

Don was always pretty well organized. He has a great memory and was definitely five steps ahead of the game. Still trying to think of something new. He wanted the shop to be changing and looking fresh in some way. We did some sort of a remodel about every 10 years, the first one being in 1985, then 1995, 2005, and 2015. He had a vision, and it always seemed to help the business grow.

FAMILY BUSINESS

My first impression was that he was very nice to me and to everyone he met. I mean, genuinely nice without any façade. He was always thinking about helping others. Whenever a peddler would come in off the street, Don would buy two or three of whatever they had and give them to the employees. He knew I liked to cook, and I still use the stainless steel salad bowl he gave to me when I first started there in November of 1978. Occasionally, someone (usually a homeless person) would be sitting on the porch at the shop, and Don would think nothing of giving the guy $20.00 for food. I have often used this term to describe him; "He has a heart as big as Montana."

I had been working for him a few months, and my little Datsun needed a significant repair. I was at Hansen's when the mechanic called at work to tell me it would be over $600.00. My eyes welled up with some fat tears. Don called me up to his office and said, "I can't stand to see a woman cry," before he paid for my repairs. He called it a bonus for doing a good job. I also remember having some great talks with him, and he often told me what his friend, Mr. Driver, used to say. Mr. Driver had told Don that even if you didn't like someone, you could always find at least one thing nice to say about them. He lived that way, and I have never forgotten it.

Closing the shop [due to the Coronavirus] has been hard for me because, being a mother, I worry about everything and everyone. It's my usual state of affairs. A lot of the "kids" (my co-workers) have been here a long time, and I am usually the employee "advocate," so I just want to make sure they will all be okay. Because they are good planners, the Hansen's have always done their best to help everyone as much as possible, sometimes even the folks they have had to let go. Julie and Shirley have been with Don for nearly 44 years, and I will have been there 42 years this year [2020] in November. The business has gone up and down, and there have been some trying times. In the old days, when we sometimes had to hold back paying vendors for a while. I would call everyone to extend due dates every Christmas, but we always paid them. They knew then and know now, we will always come through.

Probably one of the most challenging times I shared with Don was when he decided to put his youngest son, Sage, in rehab in another state. Sage had problems for years, and Don was always there for him. It was tough seeing Don wonder if he had been a good dad. Anyone who knew him realized he definitely was.

A few years later, when Sage was again in and out of rehab, Don looked at me and said, "I have done everything I can, La. I have to let him go on his own now. Otherwise, I am just enabling him." Those were hard words for him to speak. Don, who was our "rock of Gibraltar," was brought to tears by that decision.

We've had hundreds of employees come, go, come back again and go again. The fantastic thing is that several employees still come back to visit and always tell me how great it was to work here and be with the Hansen family. And it really is a family for everyone involved.

When Don finally sold his shares in Ocean pacific, we were seated in his office talking, and I asked him how it felt to be in the millionaire's club. He looked at me and said he didn't feel any different. He realized money didn't bring happiness, and as long as he had enough to live on, the rest didn't really matter. Money didn't change the way he lived. It was clear he had come from a family where he had to work hard for everything and was always grateful for what he had, no matter what.

People often ask me what I'm most proud of, and it's that I've given a lot of young people a start in life. I remember most of their faces because I've always tried to get to know my employees, see what they need, what they do, and who their parents are. I've had some of my best ideas from people, the gardener. Patty Bolton gave us the best marketing idea

FAMILY BUSINESS

we've ever had. It's called "Goods for Grades," where we give away products to kids in exchange for their grades. It's been one of our most successful ventures. We've had employees work for us over the years, and I'm always gratified when someone comes in and says, "I don't know if you remember me, but I worked for you once, and it really helped me. "

While longtime Hansen employee Patty Bolton was not born into the Hansen family, she feels connected as if she were. According to her:

Hansen's is my home and has been home to a lot of people. There are over half a dozen folks here who've been here 20 years or more. In part, that's because the Hansen family doesn't just hire you; you become part of a family that supports you with more than just a paycheck.

Not many kids were shopping at Hansen's in 1995 when I started and thought of "Goods for Grades." It was a way of rewarding kids and getting them into the shop. Boy, did it work! I believe we have given over a

> million dollars in Goods for Grades vouchers since it began.
>
> Don has made an impression on me that will stay with me my entire life. The way he does business, the way he treats his employees. He is an inspiration, and I truly love that man.

Josh Hansen was raised in Montana in response to wanting a break from Southern California's overcrowding and parental concern for the party scene destroying so many young people, especially in Southern California beach towns. The three of them moved to the remote town of Big Sky, where Josh lived until the age of 22.

According to Josh:

> My dad instructed me about many things over a long period. Mainly after we moved to Big Sky when I was 10. Before that, I didn't see him much because he worked a lot. His main messages to me never changed: Be honest,

have integrity, work hard, always treat others with respect, have common sense, and maintain a sense of humor.

He taught me all about hunting, the outdoors, and horses. We hunted off the horses most of the time, and I spent many days with him on his horses. I shot my first bull elk with my dad on a day when we each shot an elk. That was a great moment for both of us, as it is hard to take down an elk.

Horses have been an essential part of his life and mine since I was really young. When I got into skydiving, that was a little different. I started 40 years after him and had seen all the pictures and heard all the stories of his exploits. It has been enjoyable to share all of our common experiences in the sport of skydiving.

Growing up in Montana, most of my friends had no idea what the family did. Once I told them, they all thought that was pretty cool because surfing was so popular and was growing so fast. I was lucky to have the best mentor and dad in the world. He taught me so many life lessons and always encouraged me to do the right thing even if it did not benefit me. He said that if you put your head down and work hard, it will work out. He wasn't really strict, and he was even-tempered, but if you crossed him, he would let you know. The belt only came out once, and I think that was just a scare tactic.

Running the store has been pretty organic over the past five to seven years. My dad always told me to use common sense as the foundation in business. He said I should surround myself with people smarter than me, treat those around me as well as possible, and be honest and fair. He is a handshake kind of guy. If you shake on it, he'll honor his word and expect you to keep yours. I have really tried to be that kind of guy as well.

I was lucky that he had been successful enough to spend a lot of time with me as a youngster, and he was fortunate to have an amazing wife (my mom) who helped raise me. The two of them gave me a fantastic upbringing that I am forever grateful for. I could

FAMILY BUSINESS

not have asked for better parents. We have a fantastic family, very flawed, like all families, but when the chips are down, we come together with love and support.

I've always enjoyed going out to eat with the family, but Dad wouldn't often order anything when we did. He would say he wasn't hungry, but he would pick off everyone else's plate when the food came. When he got home, he would say, "I didn't eat anything." I'd say, "Dude, you ate more than if you had ordered your own plate; you ate everyone else's food." [Laughs]

Recently, a buddy and I were in Montana, hunting elk. We had all of our gear brought in on horseback, hiked in behind the riders, and set up a wall tent. We'd been in there a week and had plans for the guide, a friend of ours, to ride in, pick up our gear and ride us out. The guy in charge of taking our gear out had slid off a roof and busted his heel. He called a buddy, Charley Immenschuh, and they coordinated to meet at the trailhead and ride in.

Somehow they didn't quite connect, and their messages got crossed, so they weren't going to be there.

We had taken down the camp, got all the horses packed up, and started cruising out. It's in the fall, there's nobody around, and we're in grizzly country. I don't feel that comfortable being in an area like that alone. Most of the fish and game guys will recommend you always hunt with someone else. We come around the corner, and guess who's riding up the trail at 83 years old by himself? My friend Casey turns to me and says, "Is that your dad?" I turned to him and said, "Yeah, that's my dad."

THE CO-AUTHORS JOURNEY

My second and third surfboards were Hansen's, possibly shaped, glassed, sanded, and polished by the man himself in the early '60s. I like to think so anyway. On those boards, I went from a crouching kook to a decent surfer, turning, cutting back, and occasionally hanging five.

While I loved my Hansen surfboards, the name meant nothing more to me than those of Ford or Levi. It was a brand completely disassociated in my mind from an actual person. It would be years before I realized the board maker's full name, Don Hansen, or, as it states on his birth certificate, Donald Milton Hansen. This was a real person with a real story, an amazing story that needed telling, especially in times like these, when many lack hope and common sense and seem to have lost their way. While far from perfect by his own admission, Don stayed pretty much

HANSEN

true to the path he began on while helping others find it as well.

When I moved to Encinitas in 1970, I often frequented Hansen Surfboards. It was different than the average surf shop of the time. Instead of some scruffy surfer dude dripping saltwater onto a ragged carpet, there were pretty salespeople and everything neatly displayed for the active beachgoer. There were also surfboards lined up like so many spit-shined lollypops, and sold by some of the best surfers in town. There were surf trunks, walk shorts, and even snow skis for those willing to drive two hours to Big Bear in the winter. Photos of surf heroes Mike Doyle, Rusty Miller, Linda Benson, and Margo Godfrey lined the walls, along with museum-quality surfboards from the distant past.

Sometime after my first visit, I got a job in the Hansen factory in Solana Beach, where the first molded surfboards were being produced. Hollow boards were all the rage at the time, even though a hidden design flaw would soon sink them. The seal binding the

THE CO-AUTHOR'S JOURNEY

boards would sometimes crack, causing them to fill with water. My own test run ended after a few rides on what initially felt like a good board. Then, without warning, a leaky seam nearly sent the experimental stick to the seafloor. While the process was not yet perfected, Hansen proved to be about 40 years ahead of his time.

Don Hansen was friendly but serious as he carefully inspected our work before it was sent out for sale. Still, I knew little about him, as we had never shared a meal or a wave in the Swami's lineup. There were, however, increasingly faint rumblings that he had once been a big-wave charger who now spent his free time jumping from airplanes. That was my first hint that his calm exterior disguised a wild side.

Over the next 50 years, I would encounter Hansen, not in the ocean or on some hellish adventure, but peacefully walking the beach as he does now with his two rescue dogs, Fred and Barney.

I was living in Cardiff a few years back when my neighbor, Gary Stewart, reminded me of Hansen's story and suggested I write his biography. At Gary's prompting, I drafted a proposal and dropped it on Don's doorstep. About a week later, I got a call from him saying he was interested and wanted to meet. The first meeting was with Don and his son and store manager, Josh. They liked the idea, but Don, in what I would soon discover was his typically humble manner, wondered aloud if anyone would want to read about his life. Plus, he was busy helping run the store part-time and driving back and forth to their second home in Big Sky, Montana, with his wife, Shirley

    I learned that Don was a deeply caring man who adored and was adored by his family, many friends, and employees, some who have been with him for over 45 years. In his office, photos and awards offering testimony to a life of high adventure are displayed next to family snapshots of birthdays and weddings. He had been to the top of two adrenaline-charged sports: big wave surfing and skydiving. He had won two rodeos as a team roper at an age when his contemporaries were stuck deep in the folds of the lazyboy with a firm grip

THE CO-AUTHOR'S JOURNEY

on nothing more challenging than a remote control or a beer.

It's been decades since I was a wide-eyed gremmie listening to tales by legendary surfers like Dale Velzy or Donald Takayama. Still, this past year I often found myself seated like a young surfer around a fire ring, hearing bigger than life stories fueled by equal parts adrenaline, business sense, and care for others. I paid particular attention whenever Don laughed and flashed that youthful smile, a sure tip that slices of his colorful and unique life were on his mind.

From Hansen's front room overlooking Cardiff Reef, Don looked out remembering all the years he's watched the various moods of that wave and the community that grew up around it. According to him, "I used to lifeguard here, and I surfed here a lot, but I have never seen it as good as it is now. Not long ago, I sat up in my bedroom and saw the best surf I had ever seen here. To me, it looked exactly like Sunset Beach in Hawaii. The offshore wind was howling, and it was really hollow, big, and perfect. It was huge, and I remembered that you don't need to be in Hawaii to enjoy a great ride or to get worked. Some of these places in Encinitas can give you a thrill and hammer you hard. I've had amazing waves and been hammered here and at Swami's a few times on big north swells."

Knowing that the ocean tells only a portion of the story, I recently drove to the Hansen home in Big Sky, Montana. Along the way, I stopped in Scipio, Utah, a blink of a town where Don sat in a thunderstorm 60-some years ago while hitchhiking to his new home in California.

Montana is a deep and wide territory containing more than meets the eye. It was there, at home with Don, Shirley and their mutts, Fred and Barney that I sat with Don on his deck above the Gallatin River's middle fork, as rushing water electrified his words. He drove me into Yellowstone National Park one morning where a herd of 40 buffalo was roaming free, and I contemplated a time when the entire country was wild and how some things, like the man seated next to me, refused to be completely tamed.

THE CO-AUTHOR'S JOURNEY

This was a cerebral journey unlike any I would attempt in the flesh—riding 20 foot-plus waves, falling to earth at 120 miles per hour, and roping steers on the back of a charging horse. I am grateful for the privilege of coming along for the ride. The sea, the mountains, big skies, family, friends, and faith have helped shape Don Hansen into a man like none I have ever known.

Chris Ahrens

ACKNOWLEDGMENTS

To my best friend, Terry Fisher. Since most of our exploits were X-rated, I didn't mention them in these pages. To Bruce Walton, Brooks Gifford, Patty Fisher, Ron Smith, Bill and Lynn White, Barry Doell, Fred Smole, Roger Maxey, Brian Sipe, Mary Lynn Weitzen, Sandy Driver, Jeff Adams and Geoff Bell. My apologies to you for not having room in this book to tell about all the great times we had. Here's to you and those others whose names didn't make it into print. Until then, I look forward to many more great adventures together.

-Don Hansen

The book, *Hansen* can be purchased directly at

Hansen Surfboards
1105 S. Coast Highway 101
Encinitas, CA 92024
Or by visiting our website:
www.hansensurf.com

To contact Perelandra Publishing Inc. or *Hansen* co-author, Chris Ahrens, drop a note to: Perelandrapub@gmail.com

Perelandra Publishing Inc.
perelandrapublishing.com